TRANS

Exploring Gender Identity and Gender Dysphoria

– a guide for everyone (including professionals)

Ed. Az Hakeem

THE EDITOR

Dr Az Hakeem (MBBS, FRCPsych, Msc M.InstGA) is a top gender expert. He is a Consultant Psychiatrist and Visiting Professor in Psychiatry & Applied Psychotherapy. He ran a specialist Gender Dysphoria service in the NHS for 12 years. He now practises in the private sector at The Priory Hospital Roehampton and at Harley Street. He is a Visiting Professor at Bradford University and a Senior Clinical Lecturer at The University of New South Wales, Australia.

Az has a wealth of media experience. He was an on-screen resident psychiatrist alongside Davina McCall on Channel 4's *Big Brother*, and a psychotherapist and co-presenter on E4's *Wife Swap: The Aftermath*. He has also appeared as Resident Psychiatrist on *Weekend Sunrise* in Australia and GMTV in the UK.

First published in Great Britain 2018 by Trigger Press

Trigger Press is a trading style of Shaw Callaghan Ltd & Shaw Callaghan 23 USA, INC.

The Foundation Centre
Navigation House, 48 Millgate, Newark
Nottinghamshire NG24 4TS UK

www.trigger-press.com

British Library Cataloguing in Publication Data

A CIP catalogue record for this book is available upon request from the British Library

ISBN: 978-1-911246-49-7

This book is also available in the following e-Book formats:

MOBI: 978-1-911246-52-7
EPUB: 978-1-911246-50-3
PDF: 978-1-911246-51-0

Cover design and typeset by Fusion Graphic Design Ltd

Project Management by Out of House Publishing

Printed and bound in Great Britain by Bell & Bain, Glasgow

Paper from responsible sources

TRIGGERPRESS

Giving mental health a voice

**Thank you for purchasing this book.
You are making an incredible difference.**

At least 50% of Trigger Press proceeds go directly
to The Shaw Mind Foundation.

The Shaw Mind Foundation is a charity that focuses entirely on mental
health and was set up by Adam Shaw in order to open conversations
around the globe to support sufferers. It is the parent organisation to
Trigger Press, and a large proportion of the proceeds from the books
published go to it. To find out more about The Shaw Mind Foundation
www.shawmindfoundation.org

MISSION STATEMENT

*Our goal is to make help and support available for every
single person in society, from all walks of life.
We will never stop offering hope. These are our promises.*

Trigger Press and The Shaw Mind Foundation

the *Shaw* mind
FOUNDATION

Supporting children, adults and families
for better mental health. #letsdostuff

WARNING: This book contains graphic images.

CONTENTS

SECTION I
GENDER DYSPHORIA TERMINOLOGY

SECTION 2
UNDERSTANDING GENDER DYSPHORIA

SECTION 3
CHANGING SEX

SECTION 4
MEASURING GENDER DYSPHORIA
AND TREATMENT OUTCOMES

SECTION 5
TRANSGENDER POLITICS

APPENDIX

ACKNOWLEDGEMENTS

Fintan B Harte
MA, MB, BCh, Dobs, DCH, FRCPsych, FRANZCP

Fintan Harte is a Consultant Psychiatrist with over twenty years' experience as a gender specialist working in transgender health. He has been Head of Unit, Monash Gender Dysphoria Clinic, and is now in private practice at the Albert Road Clinic, Melbourne. He is a member of WPATH and current President of ANZPATH – Australian and New Zealand Professional Association for Transgender Health.

Andrew Ives M.B., CHB, FRACS

Andrew Ives is a qualified Plastic and Reconstructive Surgeon based in Melbourne. He has been performing transgender surgery for the past seven years. He qualified from Liverpool Medical School UK in 1989, and then emigrated to Australia, where he reviewed his postgraduate training in Plastic and Reconstructive surgery. He worked in Queensland for ten years in private practice, before returning to Melbourne to pursue his interest in transgender surgery. He is also the Deputy Director of the Victorian Adult Burns Service at the Alfred Hospital.

Rosemary Anne Jones M.B. Ch.B. FRCOG, FRANZCOG

Born in England Rosemary trained in Obstetrics and Gynaecology in Natal, and thereafter at Groote Schuur Hospital in Cape Town. She then obtained her Membership in the Royal College of Obstetricians and Gynaecologists in London.

After emigrating to Australia, Rosemary took up a position as a Senior Visiting Specialist at the Queen Elizabeth and Queen Victoria Hospitals in Adelaide in 1979, while starting a private practice. For 30 years now, she has taken an increasing interest in the problems of the menopause, laparoscopic surgery and the treatment of gender dysphoria, both surgical and hormonal. She herself underwent surgical reassignment in September 2007 and lives contentedly with another woman. She has a current passion for the treatment of premenstrual tension syndrome.

Elizabeth Riley PhD, MA(Couns), BSc

A Sydney-based counsellor, academic & clinical supervisor specialising in gender identity who has worked exclusively with trans clients and their families for nearly 20 years. Elizabeth has a PhD titled 'The needs of gender variant children and their parents' (2012), and provides training in gender diversity and dysphoria regarding children and young adults for service providers and schools where children are undergoing a social gender transition. Elizabeth has published many papers and book chapters on the needs of children with gender diversity and the assessment of adolescents with gender dysphoria.

Melissa Vick B.A., B.Mus., Dip.Ed., M.Ed., PhD.

Melissa Vick spent most of her working life as a teacher, researcher and scholar at James Cook University, Australia. Her research has traversed the disciplines of history, sociology and philosophy, in fields as diverse as education, road safety and trans wellbeing, focusing on social norms and their policing, marginalized social groups, and professionalism.

She transitioned relatively late, at age 62, remaining, with strong support from key colleagues, in her academic position until her retirement in late 2012. She enjoys an extensive international network of friends, and is actively involved in mentoring, supporting and advocating for trans people.

Kevan Wylie MD FRCP, FRCPsych, FRCOG, FECSM

Kevan is a Consultant in Sexual Medicine, Porterbrook Clinic, Sheffield; Honorary Professor of Sexual Medicine, University of Sheffield; and President at the World Association for Sexual Health. Since 1999, he has worked full time in sexual medicine for the UK National Health Service. He is Clinical Lead at the Porterbrook Clinic (sexual medicine, psychosexual and relationship psychotherapy, and transgender services) and Consultant Lead for andrology (urology) at the Royal Hallamshire Hospital.

Kevan has been a member of several UK and European advisory groups for the assessment and management of the spectrum of sexual and gender issues in women and men. He chaired the UK intercollegiate committee on good practice guidelines for individuals with gender dysphoria issued in 2013 and was a member of the WPATH committee for Standards of Care for the Health of Transsexual, Transgender, and Gender-Nonconforming People,

Version 7. In September 2012, Kevan became the president of the World Association for Sexual Health.

Luka Griffin

Luka Griffin is a young transgender man, living in North Queensland, Australia. In November 2016, Luka was the first transgender teen in North Queensland to succeed in securing testosterone treatment through the Family Court process, setting a vital precedent for future transgender youth wishing to access necessary hormones in regional Queensland. His case was also used to highlight the issues within Australia's legal system towards transgender youth. Looking ahead, Luka wishes to continue advocating for the rights of transgender youth in Australia.

DISCLAIMER

From the outset, let's acknowledge that trans terminology is contentious.

Originally the language of trans was dictated by people outside the trans community. For example, terms like "sex change" were coined by medical professionals and have since come to be seen as divisive by some people. But subsequently, the trans community has taken ownership of the language that people use to talk about trans issues – and rightfully so. As a result, the language has evolved – and keeps evolving.

This does mean that it's hard to reach a consensus on what is and isn't acceptable terminology. The trans community is not a homogenous group. Different people with different experiences, and different preferences have equally different takes on what is and isn't acceptable.

In deciding what terminology to use in this book, I had two main concerns:

1. To ensure that the book was accessible to as wide a readership as possible.

2. To use the words and terminology that the people I interact with professionally and personally are comfortable with.

I acknowledge that some people will take exception with some of the terms I have used. And if there is terminology in this book that doesn't chime with your own preferences, I hope you'll appreciate that I have not tried to offend. Indeed, there is not a general consensus, even among the authors who have collaborated with me on this book – and we have certainly had some good debates on the subject.

So while it is not possible (and may never be possible) to find a terminology that everyone accepts and endorses, I do believe that this process of talking about trans issues – and what is and isn't acceptable language – plays an important part in making trans issues more readily understood by the wider community.

INTRODUCTION

The aim of this book is to help everyone understand gender dysphoria and related concepts. It isn't just for professionals, and it isn't just for people who have a gender dysphoria. This book will be of use to the family members of people with a gender dysphoria, their friends, colleagues, and anyone who would appreciate some help in untangling the differing terms. Put simply, this book will explain what gender dysphoria is, how it affects people, and what is on offer medically, surgically, and psychotherapeutically for people with gender dysphoria.

I trained in medicine as a doctor and then as a psychiatrist. Subsequently, I trained as a psychoanalytic psychotherapist, and then as a group analyst. I have had patients with gender dysphoria in all of my clinical roles, including as a junior doctor in plastic and reconstructive surgery where I was able to assist in surgical sex-reassignment procedures. Most of my clinical work in gender dysphoria has been as a medical psychotherapist and I operated a specialist service in the UK NHS for over 12 years, offering specialist psychotherapy for people with a gender dysphoria, establishing a detailed understanding of each person over regular weekly sessions over a number of years. Since then I have continued this work in the private sector. It is through this detailed psychotherapeutic work over many years that my understanding of gender dysphoria was informed, then over-hauled, and then further refined and fine-tuned, and I am immensely grateful to all the wonderful patients I have worked with.

I am also hugely grateful to my colleagues who have made such fascinating contributions to this book:

Elizabeth Riley has provided an insight into the psychological challenges faced by parents of a child identifying as trans. Kevan

Wylie and Fintan Harte's chapters will be helpful to anyone wanting to get their head around what services are on offer from Gender Identity Services. Rosemary Jones has explained how hormones are used for physical gender transition and has provided a 'maintenance guide' as how to best look after a neo-vagina for a post-operative trans woman with the kind of tips that you probably won't find printed anywhere else.

Andrew Ives took time out of his extremely busy surgical practice to provide us with a step-by-step guide to surgical gender transition. I believe this will de-mystify what happens during surgical sex-reassignment procedures, and shed some light on what is possible, what the limitations of surgery are, and what may be expected from a surgical perspective if this is being considered. Melissa Vick and Luka Griffin have shared their own personal experiences of gender transitioning, Luka doing this early in life, and Melissa much later. Melissa's overview of trans politics will give you a sense of just how politically charged, and at times conflictual, the trans arena is with professionals, trans persons, and 'the community'.

I would like to thank the many people who have made significant contributions from the Australia and New Zealand Professional Association for Transgender Health (ANZPATH), whom I befriended during a working sabbatical in Australia. I would also like to thank my research team at the University of New South Wales. I wanted to use an outcome measuring tool for use in Gender Dysphoria and its treatment, but it didn't exist. So they painstakingly helped me devise the GPSQ, and helped conduct the accompanying research.

The GPSQ is the world's first measuring tool for clinicians and researchers for detecting Gender Dysphoria and assessing its response to any intervention (whether that intervention be psychological, hormones, surgery or anything else) which, uniquely, is not based in an outdated binary framework of gender. The GPSQ can be used with people of any gender identity, including those with non-binary gender identities, gender-queer, gender-neutral or people identifying as intersex. We wanted the GPSQ to be free to use and readily available, and I encourage anyone who may find it useful to use the version in this book. (And I welcome any offers of ongoing research with the GPSQ.)

People with gender dysphoria often find themselves misunderstood: by friends, colleagues, family, professionals and, sometimes along the way, by themselves. I hope this book may help replace misunderstanding with understanding.

SECTION 1
GENDER DYSPHORIA TERMINOLOGY

CHAPTER 1

SEX, GENDER AND SEXUALITY

SEX

Sex is the word used to describe someone's *biological* sex. It is determined by chromosomes and physically manifests itself through the body. Three categories exist: male, female, and intersex.

The male sex results from XY sex chromosomes and displays male anatomical sex organs, irrespective of psychological gender role or identity.

The female sex results from XX sex chromosomes and displays female anatomical sex organs irrespective of psychological gender role or identity.

Intersex is an umbrella term for persons whose chromosomes and / or physical bodies do not fit into either of the above categories. It is estimated that approximately 1 in 200 babies are born with an intersex condition. A person with an intersex condition may have differing combinations of sex chromosomes (such as XXY or XXX or XO) or their bodies may have developed atypical responses to a sex hormone. The end result differs in accordance to the exact type of intersex condition. Examples include people who may have the external appearance of belonging to one biological sex but have the internal sex organs of the other, or persons who have ambiguous or undifferentiated genitalia making it difficult to designate them as biologically male or female at birth.

Historically, people born with intersex conditions have been raised in either the male or female role. Growing up in a society where most people are perceived as either one or other of the two sexes, it was thought by parents and medical professionals that it would be less confusing for that individual. This presumption has raised some controversy within the adult intersex community. Some intersex adults have expressed regret at having been assimilated into the male or female gender. Opinions remain divided on the issue.

GENDER

Unlike 'sex', which is a biological characteristic manifested in bodies and determined by chromosomes, 'gender' is a psycho-social construct without any location in the body. Gender relates to psychological, behavioural, and social characteristics attributed to a particular sex, as perceived by a person or the society they live in. It is my opinion that gender has no biological or genetic basis within the individual, and is reliant on a societal context in order to have meaning, although I am sure plenty of other gender specialists may disagree.

A **gender role** is assigned when we associate certain attributes, behaviours, clothes, activities or toys with either males or females, not because there is anything about our male or female chromosomes linking us to those things, but because society has associated them with those sexes. In some societies, it may be considered feminine to wear high heeled shoes, lipstick, and have long hair, whilst in other societies it may be considered feminine to have a shaved head or a neck extended by a series of metal circles.

When a child or adult shows an interest in something which we have identified as more commonly associated with the other sex or shows a lack of interest in something we'd expect them to be interested in, we may be in danger of deducing they have a problem with their gender identity. Fortunately, this kind of thinking is less common today. Girls can play football and boys can play with dolls without their parents necessarily convincing themselves – or convincing the child – they have an issue with their gender identity.

Gender Identity is the sense one has of one's own gender and what we identify ourselves as. This may not correspond with how other people perceive our gender or with the biological sex of our body or chromosomes.

Up until recently, most people limited their understanding of gender to a binary repertoire, corresponding to the two biological sexes of male and female. There has now been a growing awareness of gender identities existing outside of the binary male / female framework. Increasing numbers of people do not feel that the existing male / female framework is one in which they are able to are able to fit and, as such, are experimenting with identities that serve to subvert it. These individuals may identify themselves as 'gender-queer' as derived from 'queer theory', which is a socio-political term used by a number of writers, such as Judith Butler.

EXAMPLES

Jane considered herself a 'very girly' female, and, as a young girl, loved anything to do with princesses, fairies, and the colour pink. As she grew older, she identified with what she considered a very stereotypical feminine identity within a western society.

John identified himself with what he considered a very masculine gender identity. As a young boy he enjoyed playing with toy guns and military action figures. As an older child he was a keen rugby player, and as an adult, he went to work as a city banker and prided himself in wearing sharp tailored suits.

Juno is a biological female in that she was born a girl. As she got older she increasingly identified herself as gender-neutral. As a teenager, she identified herself as asexual and adapted her appearance accordingly. She was often presumed by others to either be a 'goth' or a 'punk' due to her unique appearance. She tries to avoid conforming to gender stereotyped attributes which she identifies as either being strongly male or female. Instead, she strives to adopt a gender-neutral identity and appearance. She shaves her head and wears make up but not in a manner which would be considered stereotypically 'feminine'.

Xave is a biological male in that he was born a boy. As an adult, he identifies himself as gender queer. Unlike Juno who avoids gender-stereotyped attributes, Xave tries to combine what he believes to be stereotypically male and female characteristics in his appearance and behaviour. By combining both stereotypical male and female components in his identity, Xave hopes that he will challenge the preconceptions of those around him about what it is to be male or female.

SEXUALITY

Unlike sex and gender which both pertain to characteristics of ourselves, sexuality refers to what we are attracted to (in most cases, outside of ourselves). Sexuality is essentially what a person is sexually excited by, irrespective of what / who they are themselves.

Statistically most people are sexually attracted to persons of the opposite sex which leads many people to believe that a person's sexuality is determined by their own biological sex. Another common misunderstanding is the presumption that everyone has a sexuality directed to either the opposite sex (heterosexual) or the same sex (homosexual, gay, lesbian) or both (bisexual). The reality is that a person may have a sexuality directed to almost anything or in some cases, nothing at all.

Most people find that their sexual preferences become fixed and unchangeable by early adulthood and there is no evidence that this is likely to change, even if the person or society would like this to happen. In the last century, prior to the gay rights movement and the legalisation of homosexuality, there were attempts to change a person's sexuality via various means, including aversion therapy or psychotherapy. Many years ago, it was thought that if an aversive stimulus was given to someone, e.g. an electrical charge or chemically induced nausea at the same time as being shown images which they would usually find pleasurable or exciting, then the person may be re-trained to find such images / ideas as "aversive" rather than pleasurable. There is no evidence to suggest that any such interventions had any intended effect.

While most of us would consider such interventions to be grossly unethical, there are, unfortunately, still some people who seek them, and some psychotherapists who erroneously believe they will work. More recently, similar attempts have been made to change the sexuality of persons with societally unacceptable desires, such as those who are only attracted to persons under the legal age of consent or only excited by certain scenarios such as extreme non-consensual violence. Whilst there is some proof that certain interventions can reduce a person's libido or their likelihood of acting out such sexual acts, there is scant evidence that therapeutic interventions can change their sexual preference once it has become set as an adult.

While sexuality is usually directed towards another person, some people may instead be stimulated by 'things' or concepts instead. Examples include people who are primarily sexually excited by animals, cars, violence, captivity, asphyxiation, and other scenarios which may or may not involve other persons.

Some individuals are primarily sexually attracted to clothing which they associate with the opposite sex (fetishistic transvestites) or with the imagined concept of themselves as having bodily parts associated with the opposite sex (autogynaephilia in men and autoandrophilia in women). Both of these conditions will be described in more detail later in this book.

Some individuals are not sexually attracted to either males or females, but as they have never experienced sexual attraction to another person, they may not be aware of its absence. This is similar to a person not realising that they are colour-blind if they have never had the experience of perceiving colour. A person may physically go through the mechanical motions of sexual intercourse without experiencing either excitement or aversion. As they are capable of going through the motions of sexual intercourse, achieve physical orgasm, and reproduce, they may be mistaken by others, including their sexual partners, as having a particular sexuality. However, the absence of any internally experienced erotic desire differentiates them from those with a sexual desire associated with the actions they are able to mechanically fulfil. Such individuals may be asexual and without any sexual desire or have sexual desires directed towards non-person related areas.

EXAMPLE

Michael is a 34 year-old male. He has never been overly interested in having sex with either men or women. He could not really get what all the fuss was about when he and his friends were going through puberty and everyone else seemed to be very excited about their newly discovered sexualities. Michael has never had any sexual fantasies about men or women. While Michael is not particularly sexually aroused by either men or women, neither is he particularly revulsed by the idea of sex with people either.

He met Mandy in his late twenties. All his friends were getting married and Michael found that his friends were less available to hang out with him. Mandy immediately got on well with Michael. He was handsome, fun to be around, and they shared similar interests. Mandy and Michael started a relationship and later got married and had two children together. Michael is able to physically have sex with Mandy although he is not particularly into it, he is not averse to it either. He has sex when Mandy wants to, as he is aware that is what Mandy wants. As Michael is married to a woman and has produced children from their sexual activity together, everyone presumes that Michael is heterosexual. However, while Michael has physically managed to function in a heterosexual manner, the complete absence of sexual interest and arousal suggests that Michael is actually asexual rather than heterosexual.

CHAPTER 2

TRANSSEXUAL, TRANSGENDER, AND GENDER DYSPHORIA

TRANSSEXUALITY

 Transsexualism is the desire to live and be accepted as a member of the opposite sex, usually accompanied by a sense of discomfort with one's anatomic sex.

People identified or identifying as transsexual may have had gender reassignment surgery, cross-sex hormone treatment or may not want to have physical interventions such as hormones or surgery. The word transsexual indicates that there are bodily changes in relation to one's sex which the individual feels are needed due to a discordance with their experienced gender identity. While gender is absent from the term, a conflict between one's gender identity and physical sex are necessary for the condition.

Whilst many people in the world have rallied against societal gender stereotyping, it has been argued that central to the notion of transsexualism is a rigid adherence to perceived gender role characteristics, behaviours, and conventions, even if these correspond to a sex differing to one's biological sex. Such a slavish adherence is in an attempt to comply with perceived gender rules, to fit in and 'pass'.

Some transsexual persons identify themselves as transsexual and are comfortable with being identified as transsexual. Many prefer to be perceived as non-transsexual members of the sex with which they identify. This is referred to as 'passing' as a member of that sex. This may be preferred as it is considered to be safer than to be identified as transgender.

The term **pre-operative transsexual** refers to someone identifying as transsexual, but who has not had gender-reassignment surgery.

They may be living in a cross-gendered sex role and / or taking hormones but have not had genital or breast surgery.

EXAMPLE

Justin was born male. In his twenties, he increasingly identified with a female gender role. When he was 29, he decided to live in the female gender role and changed his name to Justine. Justine's preference is to be referred to by female pronouns. She wears her clothes, hair, and make-up in a manner which she identifies as being feminine, and requests that others treat her as a female. Justine is considering whether to have female hormones and / or surgery in the future, but is undecided as to whether to proceed. Justine considers herself as a pre-operative trans female at present.

The term **post-operative transsexual** refers to someone who has had surgery to remove or reduce the secondary sexual characteristics of their biological sex and may have had surgical procedures to enable them to have the appearance of the sex they identify as. Such operations may include:

- Orchidectomy, (commonly known as castration) the removal of testicles
- Penectomy, removal of penis
- Vaginoplasty, creation of a neo-vaginal space lined by penile skin and neo-vaginal labia from scrotal skin
- Mastectomy, removal of breast tissue in women

Other maxillofacial surgical procedures may be requested such as reduction of the 'Adam's apple' in men (cricoid cartilage reduction) and jaw / chin reshaping.

You can surgically adapt the body to have the appearance of the other sex, but we can never replicate the reproductive function. In other words, it is not possible to for a man to be surgically changed into a woman who is then able to become pregnant or give birth. Neither is it possible for a female to be surgically transformed into a man who is able to produce sperm.

EXAMPLES

Alice is a 50-year-old post-operative transsexual female. She was born male and spent the first thirty years of her life as Andrew, and was happy using male pronouns, prior to embarking on a gender role transition. Initially, Andrew was referred to a specialist gender identity clinic which supervised his gender transition. Firstly, Andrew lived full time in the female gender role, changed wardrobe, and legally changed name to Alice, which was reflected on her passport and all her documents. Having changed name, Alice's preference was to be referred to by female pronouns. After living full time in the female gender role, Alice was prescribed female hormones from the gender clinic. After another few years, Alice decided to have gender reassignment surgery. The surgery involved removal of the testes and penis and refashioning of the genital area into a vaginal-like space complete with a vulva made from what had been the scrotum. Artificial breast implants gave the appearance of female breasts. Further down the line, Alice had further surgery to her face and neck area to feminise her appearance, including removal of her 'Adam's apple' and softening of her jawline. Alice identifies as a post-operative male-to-female transsexual. She is aware that although she looks convincingly female, she will not be able to become pregnant as a born-female would, but happily accepts this.

Paul is a 40-year-old post-operative female to male transsexual. Paul was born a girl and lived as Pauline until she was 20. Like Alice, Pauline also attended a gender clinic which assisted her gender transition. Paul's transition also took place through a three-stage process (previously called 'triadic therapy'): living in the opposite gender role, followed by taking hormones, and then surgery. Paul was given male hormones which caused his voice to break, and led to the development of male-pattern body and facial hair, which Paul chooses to wear as a beard. Surgery involved removal of both breasts (bilateral mastectomy) and using tissue and skin from his forearm to fashion something which could look and function almost like a penis, as well as creation of a scrotum and artificial testes. Whilst on close inspection Paul's new penis does not look or function exactly like a biological male penis and his artificial testes do not produce sperm, Paul is very satisfied with the result.

TRANSGENDER

The use of the term 'transsexual' is increasingly being replaced by 'transgender'. Whilst the term 'transsexual' has a specific definition and had previously been used for diagnostic purposes, the term transgender is less defined and more encompassing. The term is perhaps more useful than transsexual in that it at least includes reference to 'gender' which is at the core of the condition and the person's relationship to it.

Both these terms contain the prefix 'trans', which implies a switching between two binary poles (male to female or female to male). While this has been mainly the case with transsexualism, it is increasingly common for persons identifying as transgender to have gender identities outside of the binary repertoire of male / female. (Hence the term 'non-binary'.)

Transgender persons may adhere to stereotyped male / female roles or they may subvert these in a creative manner, and identify as gendered outside of the binary framework. Such individuals may identify as non-gendered, inter-gendered or as transgender without attempting to assimilate (or 'pass') as either conventionally male or female.

Cisgender is the term increasingly used by those in the transgender community when referring to non-trans people, i.e. individuals without a gender dysphoria, whose gender identity corresponds with their biological sex at birth.

GENDER DYSPHORIA

Gender dysphoria (from ancient Greek) means a sense of dissatisfaction or unhappiness with one's gender. One of the diagnostic guidelines for health professionals internationally is the DSM: The Diagnostic and Statistical Manual. The previous edition of DSM (DSM IV) used the term Gender Identity Disorder.

The newer edition (DSM V) replaces Gender Identity Disorder with the term 'gender dysphoria'. And it's proposed that the forthcoming ICD-11 will replace 'transsexualism' with the term 'gender incongruence'. This literally implies a gender identity which is not in accordance with one's biological sex, rather than necessarily an implication of what the gender identity is.

The other widely used classification system is the International Statistical Classification of Diseases and related Health Problems (ICD). In the most recent version of ICD, the ICD-10, the term 'Transsexualism' is used. The shift from using terms like "disorder" in the updated classification system are a welcome change for individuals who feel that "disorder" suggests a pathological description.

The changes towards gender dysphoria and gender incongruence will enable persons who are identifying with a different gender from their biological sex (but not necessarily the opposite sex) to be included. The previous diagnosis of transsexualism only encompassed people who identified with the opposite (binary) sex and nothing else.

The new updated classification will encompass those identifying as non-binary gender identities who do not fall neatly into the previous classifications.

EXAMPLE

Craig was born male and lived in the male role throughout his life. While he was married with children, Craig was not happy about being male and found it hard to identify with being male or with things which he perceived as being 'masculine'. He sometimes wished he was female but these feelings were stronger at some times than others. On some days Craig became very unhappy, and believed life would be much better if he was a woman, but these feelings lessened on other days. Craig did not think that changing his gender or sex would make him happier, and anticipated it would negatively impact on aspects of his life which he valued, such as his marriage, and family life with his children. He was also aware that his desire to be a woman changed from week to week and sometimes from day to day, and as such, he felt he was not interested in undergoing an irreversible 'sex-change'. To all his friends and family, Craig was a typical male as he never talked about his unhappiness and confusion with his gender identity, and there was nothing to suggest anything other than Craig being male. Craig has a gender dysphoria which does not fit in with a typical transsexual framework. As such, gender reassignment interventions such as hormones and surgery are not suitable options for him. Craig was referred to specialist therapy for people with atypical gender identity conditions which he found very helpful, especially as it was in a group setting with others who also had atypical gender identities / gender dysphoria of differing types.

Gender non-conformity may or may not be perceived to be a problem either for the gender non-conforming person themselves or for the society in which they live. It does not necessarily result in any suffering, and may be part of a creative act of subversion to a perceived social framework or convention.

A common feature of the accounts given by transgender persons is a sense of not fitting in with perceived 'norms' or expectations for their biological sex. Frequently cited examples include boys playing with dolls and preferring games with girls rather than the 'rough and tumble play' of other boys. Similarly, females may report the converse.

A sense of insecurity or under-confidence with regards to gender may result in some individuals coming to the conclusion that if they do not fit in with the perceived framework of gender, then something must be wrong with them. They believe that this could be rectified by correcting something about themselves. To put it simply: 'If I don't fit into the mould of what it is to be a boy, it must mean I should have been a girl.'

Clearly there are a great many people who do not fit this description. The above is clearly an over-simplification to illustrate a point. I have seen a great many people whose gender dysphoria is related to a lack of confidence relating to fitting in with the perceived framework. However, there are a great many people who are creatively challenging the confines and boundaries of the perceived frameworks in a way they find they can optimally express their own sense of personal identification. So for these people, rather than lacking confidence in gender frameworks, they have a prominent sense of confidence – and would not fit into the example I've described. On the other hand, a more gender-confident person who similarly finds that they do not fit in with a perceived gender framework, instead arrives at the conclusion that rather than the problem being located within them, it must be inherent to the framework of gender. They may be confident enough to flaunt the flawed framework in a manner which challenges our understanding.

Frameworks (such as gender) are after all only a hypothetical way of organising our world. If one does not fit into the framework, then it is a reflection of the limitations of the framework, rather than a defect of the person. Examples of such gender confidence include David Beckham and his reappropriation of the male earring and sarong, and the rise of *metrosexualism*. The metrosexual male questions the perceived framework of what is considered 'male' or 'female' in terms of clothing and grooming, while preserving their masculinity and male gender identity.

This is not to say that there are not transsexual people who are not able to subvert perceived gender expectations. Many gender confident trans people will choose to purposely adopt characteristics that they may perceive as belonging to different and mutually conflicting gender presentations in order to challenge what it means to be male or female, e.g. adopting a female presentation while retaining an Adam's apple, or retaining a deep voice. And there is an overlap here with the concepts of being gender queer.

EXAMPLE

We've already talked about Xave. He was born a male but later increasingly identified as gender-queer as he didn't feel he could identify with a binary gender framework. Xave feels that conventional interpretations of gender are limiting and does not feel the need to confine or restrict himself into pre-determined boxes or categories. Rather than feeling troubled or confused, Xave feels very comfortable in his own identity and is able to confidently experiment with societal stereotypes of gender in a creative manner. While Xave does not feel confused in himself, he aims to instil a degree of confusion in those around him with his appearance and self-presentation. He hopes to make others think about what they had previously taken for granted in terms of what it is to be male or female. In contrast to a person with gender dysphoria who may be troubled, unhappy or confused with their sense of gender, Xave has enough gender confidence in his gender-queer identity to playfully and creatively subvert his gender expression towards others.

THE RELATIONSHIP BETWEEN SEXUALITY AND TRANSSEXUALITY

Although the term transsexuality contains the suffix 'sexuality', it is not a type of sexuality. Transsexuality or Transgender is a condition of gender identity, but how do the concepts of sexuality and transgender relate to each other?

As mentioned, all evidence suggests that a person's sexuality is generally fixed by the time early adulthood is reached, and is unlikely to change or be changed. Most people who undergo sex-reassignment to change their gender will find that their sexuality (or what they are sexually attracted to) will most probably not change, even post transition (although there are no hard and fast rules about this). So a heterosexual male who is sexually attracted to females will most probably continue to be sexually attracted to women after he has transitioned into a male-to-female transsexual, making him a transsexual female lesbian. A homosexual male sexually attracted to other males will continue to be sexually attracted to males after he has transitioned to become a male-to-female transsexual who is now heterosexual in sexual orientation. The important thing to note is that what the person finds sexually exciting does not change. But if his or her own sex / gender has changed, then the term given to that sexuality will change. In short, the term given to the individual's sexuality changes in response to the change in the person's own sex, even though the actual sexuality (source of attraction) does not change.

Some individuals living the gender role which matches their sex at birth, who are sexually attracted to others of the same sex may refuse to identify as homosexual or gay. This is the case in only a small proportion of transgender people. When I have met such patients in clinical practice and asked them in their pre-transition state why they did not identify themselves as homosexual / gay despite being sexually attracted solely to members of the same sex, the most common reply was that they felt they had 'nothing in common with' or were 'unable to identify with' members of the gay community.

Of course, homosexuality is a descriptive term that is used when the sex of persons to whom one is sexually attracted corresponds with one's own sex. But the responses of people given above indicates an assumption of other meanings or attributes to being homosexual (possibly relating to presumed associations with a lifestyle or perhaps moral connotations associated with homosexuality) which there is some resistance to being identified with.

As described earlier, there are some people who are neither sexually attracted (nor sexually averse) to either sex but who may be able to mechanically go through the motions of sexual intimacy. Such individuals may feel a close friendship or degree of platonic intimacy with their partner whom they find attractive. However, erotic attraction is absent, as is sexual revulsion which may be associated with sexual activity without erotic attraction. Sexual activity may take place in order to meet the expectations of the partner or of social convention. A person who is technically asexual in relation to other people may either have a completely absent sexuality or a sexuality that is not directed towards other people.

Examples may include the man whose primary sexual fantasy and preoccupation was of himself either dressed in women's' clothes (*fetishistic transvestite*) or having female sexual organs or bodily parts (*autogynaephilia*). If such an individual also happened to undergo gender reassignment then their absence of erotic attraction for others would, of course, continue to be absent. However, in the same way that before their gender reassignment they could mechanically go through the motions of a sexual relationship, they may continue to be able to do that – only this time they may choose to do it with a partner of the opposite sex to their new reassigned sex.

As a result, it would initially appear that they had experienced a change in sexuality post gender-reassignment, but the reality for such asexual individuals is that their sexuality has not changed direction. It continues to be absent in relation to either sex, despite the person managing to go through the mechanical process of sexual intercourse with their partner, sustaining a relationship and maintaining the semblance of a sexuality. This is of course only applicable to a sub-population of the people I have assessed in clinical practice. There are many who would not identify with this description at all, and for whom it may be unfathomable to maintain the semblance of a sexual relationship in the absence of any strong feelings of sexual attraction.

Thus, the source of sexual interest (if any) is unlikely to change following gender reassignment. However, the extent of sexual desire experienced may well reduce. In biological males, the sex drive, also known as libido, is known to drastically reduce following castration. While reduction of sex drive and libido is not the reason for castration in gender reassignment surgery, it is to be expected in male to female gender reassignment, following chemical or physical castration. For many this is a side-effect of treatment which they are prepared to accept. Significant reduction or loss of sexual drive is an important consideration for biological males who seek gender reassignment for sexually driven purposes.

There is often diagnostic confusion amongst non-specialist clinicians, differentiating between those who are seeking gender reassignment due to a gender identity condition and those who are primarily sexually excited by cross-dressing (*fetishistic transvestism*) or the fantasised idea of themselves with female characteristics (*autogynaephilia*).

The sexual desire driving both these conditions will be significantly reduced or disappear following chemical or surgical castration, and as such, it is important to rule out whether a sexual impulse is the motivation for seeking gender reassignment. A biological male who has a physical sex reassignment for a purely sexually motivated purpose will experience a loss of libido, so that he no longer has any interest in having the transgender body he has now acquired. More detail will be given on both these sexually driven conditions later in this book.

CHAPTER 3

TRANSVESTITES, CROSS–DRESSERS, AND DRAG QUEENS AND KINGS

CROSS-DRESSER

 A 'cross-dresser' is a person who spends time adopting the external appearance, usually clothing, which they associate with the sex opposite to their own.

The term covers all forms of cross-gender dressing and does not imply any reason behind the behaviour. It does not necessarily mean that the cross-gender dressing is secondary to any gender identity, excitement (sexual or otherwise) or fulfilment of any urge to cross dress, although any of the above may come under this broad category. It includes the dressing in cross-gender clothing for purposes of theatre, comedy, and performance.

A transvestite is a type of cross-dresser, specifically a person who chooses to spend time dressed in clothing which they or their society perceives as being associated with the opposite gender to their own biological sex. I am not using the terms 'opposite sexed clothes' or 'clothes of the opposite sex' as such terms are inaccurate and misleading. Clothes do not of course have a sex or gender of their own. The decision as to whether a piece of clothing is associated with the male or female sex is determined by the person and their perceived consensus of the society they inhabit. A tartan skirt may be seen as 'feminine' in many contexts but may be considered 'masculine' when worn by men as a kilt. A pair of regular fit denim jeans may be perceived as female clothing if purchased from a women's' clothing store or men's clothing if purchased from a men's' store.

Transvestites may 'cross-dress' full-time or part-time, in which case they may also be referred to as 'dual-role transvestites', meaning that they live and dress in different gender roles at differing times.

The *'trans'* prefix of the word 'transvestite' gives an indication of the reliance of this activity upon a 'male / female' binary understanding of gender. Transvestism has little meaning when considered in isolation from the society in which it takes place. It relies on a degree of rigidity within that society as to what is associated with one gender or another. While the term transvestite only refers to the practice of wearing clothes usually associated with the opposite sex, it is helpful to consider differing types of transvestite with regards to the purpose of the cross-dressing.

Depending upon the intentions of the individual concerned, transvestism can be indicative of either a degree of rigidity with regards to the understanding of gender or conversely, of a creative and fluid expression of gender.

If the intention behind transvestism is to blend into society as a member of the opposite sex (referred to as 'passing'), then this suggests a reliance on a more rigid understanding of sex and gender. For such persons, to be perceived as a member of their biological sex instead of *'passing'* may be considered a highly unwanted outcome. These individuals may lack confidence in their sense of gender identity.

EXAMPLE

Brian was born male and lived as a man with friends who only knew of him as being male. Brian knew he was a man and did not identify himself as female and had no wish or desire to permanently live as a woman. However, Brian did like to spend periods of time dressing up in clothes and make up which made him appear as female to others. The experience of being perceived as a woman when he was cross-dressed in public was very satisfying for Brian, although not in a sexual manner. Brian would go to great lengths with his clothes and make-up to try and look as convincingly female as possible. Brian was very scared of being perceived as either male or a transvestite whilst he was out cross-dressed and considered himself to be in 'stealth' mode.

For others, the intention may not be to 'pass' as a member of the opposite sex. In this instance, the aim is to challenge the presumptions of others with regards to gender. Such individuals may be more confident in their own sense of gender identity in relation to their biological sex, and their cross-dressing serves as a creative or socio-political statement and challenge to those around them. There are several well-known entertainers and performers who are confident in their biological sex and gender role, whose use of cross-dressing serves to challenge the preconceived notions that society may have regarding gender, and especially binary gender rules, in a creative and thought-provoking manner.

EXAMPLE

Derek was born male, identifies himself as male and has no unhappiness or confusion relating to his sense of male gender identity. Sometimes when he goes out, Derek likes to wear full-length dresses, eye shadow, mascara, and lipstick combined with knee-length military-styled boots, and a moustache. He is not attempting to appear female. His chosen appearance is his way of challenging the preconceived gender associations he sees in society.

Another sub-category of transvestite may hope to be perceived as members of their biological sex in clothing usually associated with the opposite sex. Whilst this would be considered an unfavourable and humiliating outcome for other transvestites as described earlier, for this particular sub-group, the prospect of the humiliation from not 'passing' is the primary source of masochistic pleasure. Unsurprisingly, the masochochism is the primary feature here (as part of a sado-masochistic sexuality) and the cross-dressing is merely the means by which such humiliation and masochism may be achieved.

> **EXAMPLE**
>
> **James** was born male and identifies himself as male and has no desire to live as a woman or be identified as a woman. James experiences pleasure at cross-dressing in women's clothes in public with the intention of being perceived as a man in women's clothing. The aspect of the process which James finds fulfilling is the humiliation. Unlike transvestites who go to great lengths in order to be in 'stealth' and 'pass' as a woman, James goes to great lengths in order to achieve humiliating discovery and not 'pass'. James found that by walking past schools around closing time he experienced the most humiliation, which he found both terrifying and exhilarating at the same time. Apart from his transvestism, James also derives masochistic pleasure from other activities including bondage and sado-masochistic sexual activities with others into the 'BDSM' scene.

FETISHISTIC TRANSVESTISM

A fetishist is someone whose sexual desire is derived from an inanimate object (such as shoes), a non-genital body part (such as feet) or an activity not usually associated as a sexual activity (such as sneezing or cooking). *'Fetishistic transvestism'* refers to persons who dress in the clothing they associate with the opposite sex in order to achieve sexual excitement.

Cross-dressing can be a source of sexual excitement in different ways. For instance, there are differences in the extent to which the activity is sexually exciting, ranging from those who engage in cross-dressing once in a while to spice up their relationship, to those whose sole sexual preoccupation is cross-dressing, and who are unable to achieve sexual arousal or orgasm unless cross-dressed. The latter may find it harder to form lasting or meaningful intimate relationships with another person because their main source of sexual excitement is not their partner, but themselves, while cross-dressed. Any partner takes on the role of an accessory to this activity.

EXAMPLE

Jack was born male and identifies himself as male. He is heterosexual and enjoys a varied sex-life with his wife. Sometimes Jack enjoys wearing his wife's clothes during sex and his wife facilitates this. Jack is able to enjoy sex when there is no element of cross-dressing and it is not required for him to perform sexually. As such it only happens on some occasions.

Geoff was born male and identifies himself as male. Geoff is a fetishistic transvestite and finds sexual arousal and excitement by cross-dressing, either alone or going out in public cross-dressed. All of his sexual fantasies involve himself dressing in women's clothing.

He is able to have sexual relationships with women but the only source of sexual arousal for Geoff is wearing women's clothing. In relationships with women, Geoff waits a few weeks into the sexual relationship before he suggests to his partners the idea of him wearing some form of women's clothing during sex. Usually his partners find this initially amusing and intriguing. Some even seen it as exciting. After a period of time, Geoff usually insists on wearing women's clothing during sex and his partners find that what was at first an unusual novelty has become something which no longer interests them.

They also notice that during sex, Geoff seems far more excited and aroused by his own cross-dressing than he is by his partner who begins to feel secondary. As a result, Geoff's relationships have only been short-lived to date, which is frustrating for him.

For some fetishistic transvestites, the main source of sexual excitement is the clothing itself, rather than the wearing of the clothes on their body. This category may be further sub-divided into those who are sexually excited by whole garments, and those who are sexually excited by the material, such as the texture of the fabric. Others are excited by the feeling of the fabric against their bodies. Commonly cited is the feel of nylon tights against the skin of their legs. What I also noticed from my clinical work was that each person was usually consistent in terms of which component they found sexually arousing.

EXAMPLE

Clive is a 58-year-old biological male who has had an avid interest in women's stockings and hosiery since his adolescence. He remembers his mother's stockings from his childhood, and how she would pull them up over her legs as she was getting ready in the morning. As a teenager, he tried on his mother's stockings and found himself getting sexually aroused by this. The texture of the hosiery against his skin, and the sound and feel of the stocking as he pulled them over his legs became a source of sexual arousal for Clive, and remains his main source of sexual excitement to this day.

Table 1: *Differing types of fetishistic transvestism (more than one may apply in any individual)*

Cross dressing as a source of sexual excitement in addition to other sources of non-fetishistic sexual excitement
Cross-dressing as the only source of sexual excitement
Aspects of the clothing fabric causing sexual excitement
Specific items of clothing causing sexual excitement
Sexual excitement derived from the feel of the clothes upon the skin whilst wearing them
Sexual excitement from the fantasy of themselves as members of the opposite sex while cross-dressed
Sexual excitement from the idea of themselves as a member of their biological sex (i.e. being a man) wearing clothes associated with the opposite sex (women's' clothes).
Sexual excitement derived from being perceived by others as a member of the opposite sex 'passing' while cross-dressed.
Sexual excitement derived by the risk element of either 'passing' or 'not passing'
Sexual excitement from the prospect of being humiliated for being perceived as wearing clothing associated with the opposite sex whilst out in public (a form of masochism).

Moving the focus away from clothes and towards the person, the next category of fetishistic transvestite is those for whom the physical act of cross dressing facilitates a sexual fantasy relating to themselves as an individual or how they perceive themselves. For some it facilitates a fantasy of themselves as a member of the opposite sex, which is the source of sexual excitement. For these individuals there is an overlap with *autogynaephilia* and *autoandrophilia*. The terms will be explained later in this section.

EXAMPLE

Daniel is a 44-year-old biological male. He first started cross-dressing as a child in his mother's underwear when he was left home alone. As an adult, he continues to enjoy wearing women's underwear especially underpants, stockings and garters. He stands with his back to a mirror and then peers over his shoulder at the reflection of his back.

By doing this, Daniel is able to see an image of himself from behind in women's underwear, without any evidence of his male chest or genitalia. In this way, he is able to fantasise about himself being a woman, which he finds sexually arousing. While his sexual arousal and masturbation takes place at the front of his body, this is out of view of the image in the mirror and Daniel can keep this separate from the image he is being aroused by.

However, for others, it may be the opposite. The intention behind the cross-dressing may be to reinforce the appearance of an individual's biological sex. An example of this is the man who overcomes his perceived feelings of inadequacy in his male gender role through cross-dressing. He finds that dressing up in 'women's clothes' makes him appear 'obviously male' which not only reassures him but becomes a source of sexual satisfaction and reward.

'Cross-dressing' is of course something which men or women may do. Clothing which we may identify as 'feminine' may be more clearly identifiable as such, whereas clothes which we may associate as typically 'masculine' may be less clear. For example, a woman wearing a 'trouser suit' may be less conspicuously challenging a gender-barrier than a man in a dress. As such there may be a greater flexibility for the woman who may derive satisfaction from feeling that she is, to some extent, adopting a 'masculine' wardrobe whilst managing to be less conspicuous. So whilst cross-dressing occurs in men and women, we do tend to notice it more in men.

EXAMPLE:

Cecil is a 29-year-old biological male. He knows he is male and identifies as a male. As a young child, he was bullied at school for having a frail build and not being very interested in playing with other boys. The other children called him 'gay' although Cecil knew that he was not interested in boys sexually. Other children taunted him with names such as 'Big Girl's Blouse' or 'Nonce'. Cecil developed a degree of insecurity as to how others perceived his gender. Cecil has never had much facial hair but as an adult preferred to let his stubble remain. On occasions, he likes to go out in public wearing a women's dress with short sleeves to show his hairy arms, and a short hemline to reveal his hairy legs. When he is wearing the dress in public, the intention is not for him to 'pass' as a woman, but in fact the opposite. Cecil aims for those around him to identify him as a man in a dress and as such, 'definitely a man'.

Cecil not only finds this process of reaffirmation of his male gender a relief, but over time, it has also become sexually exciting for him.

Shifting into the interpersonal arena, the next categories of fetishistic transvestites derive sexual excitement from the effect their cross-dressing has on others who are able to observe it. For some, the excitement may come from '*passing*' as a member of the opposite sex whilst cross-dressing in public. Their satisfaction stems from the idea that, in the mind of another person, they existed as a member of the opposite sex, even if only briefly. For others, it is the risk element of whether or not they successfully '*pass*' which provides an adrenalin rush, which itself becomes sexually arousing.

During the 1970s, psychoanalyst, Mervyn Glasser suggested that the cause of excitement in males with fetishistic transvestism came from a sense of triumphing over a mother whom had been experienced as claustrophobic and smothering during childhood. He hypothesised that after a lifetime of feeling unable to get away from an ever-present and controlling maternal figure, the adult male found a physical way of mastering his childhood claustrophobia by literally *putting her on and taking her off at will*, as represented by women's clothing. His implication was that this new-found sense of symbolic control over the mother is such a relief that the excitement derived from this triumphant activity becomes sexually exciting.

Such an idea has appeared as the basis of many a novel and film, and is used in Alfred Hitchcock's *Psycho* (1960), as well as in the film, *The Silence of The Lambs* (1991). This proposed model can certainly be seen in some fetishistic transvestites (and I have assessed numerous patients who have offered this formulation of themselves). It is, however, by no means a universal formula, and I hope this section has demonstrated the complexity and diversity of the phenomenon.

DRAG KINGS AND DRAG QUEENS

A drag queen is a man who, for the purposes of theatrical entertainment or comedy, adopts the external characteristics, clothing, and paraphernalia usually associated with the female gender, in an extreme and exaggerated manner. The clothing is flamboyant, the make-up excessive, and the overall appearance much larger than life.

A drag king is a woman who similarly dresses in the external clothing and paraphernalia associated with the male gender, often adopting marked stereotyped male gender themes such as the Wild West cowboy, lumberjack clothing, and prominent facial hairpieces.

It is important to distinguish how the concept of 'drag' differs from transvestism. While transvestism usually involves attempts by the individual to conform and comply with perceived gender roles, drag aims to challenge preconceptions regarding gender.

A male transvestite may adorn a wig and a dress in his attempt to blend in, because he believes that these are the domain of womanhood. A drag queen will adorn the same items with the intention of theatrically pointing out to the audience how these adornments alone do not make him a woman.

Judith Butler describes in her book *Gender Trouble* that it is almost as if the drag queen provocatively says to society 'so you think this looks feminine?' In the past, psychoanalysts have not differentiated between transvestites and drag queens / kings. Some have even gone so far as to suggest that they are an unconscious attack against the opposite sex.

I would disagree. I believe that drag is not aimed at members of the sex individuals are dressing up as, but rather as a communication to society itself. Drag intends to make a parody of what society believes to be the domain of either gender, in order to make us realise how tenuous and ridiculous such constructs are. The drag queen may have all the accessories and paraphernalia which society uses to determine femininity, but the result is not feminine at all. Drag is a creatively subversive performance, inviting the audience to question frameworks of gender. It is perhaps a contrast to the manner in which transvestism subscribes and conforms unquestioningly to such frameworks.

CHAPTER 4

AUTOGYNAEPHILIA:
THE MEN WHO WANT VAGINAS

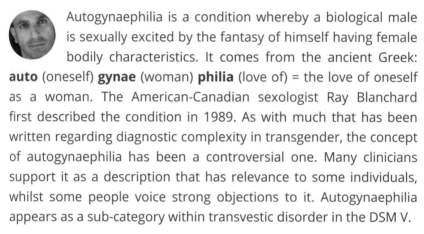Autogynaephilia is a condition whereby a biological male is sexually excited by the fantasy of himself having female bodily characteristics. It comes from the ancient Greek: **auto** (oneself) **gynae** (woman) **philia** (love of) = the love of oneself as a woman. The American-Canadian sexologist Ray Blanchard first described the condition in 1989. As with much that has been written regarding diagnostic complexity in transgender, the concept of autogynaephilia has been a controversial one. Many clinicians support it as a description that has relevance to some individuals, whilst some people voice strong objections to it. Autogynaephilia appears as a sub-category within transvestic disorder in the DSM V.

As with fetishistic transvestism, autogynaephilia is a sexually driven phenomenon. While female clothing is the source of sexual excitement in fetishistic transvestism, in autogynaephilia it is the fantasy of having female bodily characteristics. The autogynaephile may differ from the transsexual in terms of primary gender identity. Whilst the (biologically male) transsexual may identify with the female gender, the autogynaephile may identify themselves as male, but be sexually excited by the fantasy of having female bodily attributes, such as larger breasts or female genitalia. There may be an overlap with fetishistic transvestism in that cross-dressing may be employed in order to support the self-directed sexual fantasy of having a female body.

Some males fitting the description of autogynaephilia may be mistakenly diagnosed (by themselves or non-specialists) as being transsexual, and are then put forward for physical gender reassignment. The risk of genital gender reassignment surgery in these cases is of loss of sexual libido following castration, with accompanying loss of interest in the neo-vagina installed in place of the previous male genitalia. Some individuals with autogynaephilia decide to keep their male genitalia, and opt to develop a feminine body shape and breast tissue via the use of cross-gender hormones. Such individuals have been referred to colloquially as *'she-males'* in reference to the physical attributes relating to both males and females. While I have had patients who have identified with such a label, the term is understandably offensive to many.

PHYSICAL GENDER REASSIGNMENT INTERVENTIONS FOR FETISHISTIC TRANSVESTISM AND AUTOGYNAEPHILIA: A CAUTIONARY NOTE

Transvestism, fetishistic transvestism, and autogynaephilia are often mistakenly confused with transgender. The individual concerned is aware that they have an interest in wearing clothes they associate with the opposite gender or a wish for female bodily characteristics. After some self-diagnosis and internet research they often presume that such preoccupation with clothing or the body of the opposite sex suggests that they are transgender, and they may present themselves to their doctor as such and request gender reassignment. Whilst transgender and physical interventions for sex-reassignment are widely known amongst doctors of all specialties, an awareness or knowledge of other diagnoses of fetishistic transvestism and autogynaephilia are usually only limited to specialists within the field. Part of the assessment process by specialist gender services is to determine the reason behind the person's request for physical gender reassignment.

Unfortunately, people sometimes choose to bypass specialist gender services, and shop for their own quick fix from a surgeon willing to offer gender reassignment surgery. I have seen a number of patients who were referred for psychotherapy following gender reassignment surgery, which they no longer wanted after it had been carried out. Many of these people had decided that they needed to have surgical gender reassignment, and booked it (usually privately and / or in a different country) only to regret the decision upon waking from the anaesthetic. All too frequently there is a history of a sexually driven wish to change sex, secondary to fetishistic transvestism or autogynaephilia, but the libido driving this desire disappears after the castration component of gender reassignment. The end result: the person wakes up from the operation without any wish for the neo-vagina they now find in place of the male genitalia they once had.

AUTOGYNAEPHILIA CASE EXAMPLE: MR X

Mr X is a middle-aged, married man with children. He has an unremarkable male appearance and identifies himself as male. For many years, Mr X was aware of the sexual excitement he derived from fantasising about himself as a woman whilst cross-dressing, and his wife was aware of it too. At the beginning of their relationship, it would be incorporated into their sexual relationship by Mr X wearing paraphernalia he associated with the female gender, such as high heels or women's underwear. Mr X discovered 'she-male' pornography on the internet and spent increasing amounts of time looking at photographs of biological males who had a female body-shape and breasts but retained male genitalia or males with neo-vaginas. His arousal whilst viewing the pornographic material was linked to his fantasy of himself as having the breasts or vagina of a female. Mr X discussed these ongoing thoughts and fantasies with his wife. Together they concluded that as Mr X had fantasised about having a women's body for so long, he must be transgender, and his wife decided to support him in pursuing gender reassignment surgery.

Mr X decided not to go through a gender identity clinic in the public health system. It would have entailed a time-consuming process of living in the opposite gender role before cross-gender hormones, and then, eventually, the sex reassignment surgery. Instead, Mr X and his wife flew to the Far East where Mr X had booked himself in for gender reassignment surgery with a willing surgeon.

The surgical sex-reassignment surgery on Mr X's genitalia included castration and the creation of a neo-vaginal space. Immediately following his castration, Mr X lost his sexual drive and libido. He realised that despite his previous excitement at the prospect of attaining female-looking genitalia prior to his surgery, he had never identified himself as being female, despite experiencing sexual excitement from the fantasy of being female. Afterwards, he developed a profound depression concerning his surgery.

Mr X continued to live in the male gender role and felt deeply regretful and ashamed about the neo-vagina he had in place of his previous male genitalia. He was referred for psychotherapy for his depression and confusion relating to his changed wishes regarding his body, gender, and sexual drives. Careful assessment at an earlier stage may have assisted diagnosis and prevented Mr X from choosing a surgical intervention, which was not appropriate to his particular gender presentation.

AUTOANDROPHILIA

Whilst autogynaephilia, as described earlier, is the fantasy of having female bodily attributes in a biological male, autoandrophilia refers to biological women who are sexually excited at the fantasy of having male bodily attributes.

CHAPTER 5

FEMALE TO MALE: FTMs / TRANSMEN

Just as some men believe that their lives would be better if they were female, so some women believe that they should have been born as male. Previous research has suggested that transgender is three times less common in biological women. One possibility that could contribute to the difference in prevalence is that, in many societies, it is easier for women to adapt their gender role in a more masculine manner than it is for males to adopt a more 'feminine' role. Women have been wearing trouser suits since the early 20th century and *'power women'*, *'tom-boys'* and *'ladettes'* blend more into our society without their gender identity coming into question in a way that men in dresses are not able to do quite so easily. It is feasible that for many women, the ability to adopt what they consider to be a more 'masculine' role whilst still occupying their female gender identity suffices, and for them there is no need for a more extreme or visible physical transition of gender.

For those who do decide that a change of physical sex is necessary, the physical means of bodily change involves hormones and surgery, as with male to female transsexuals. The addition of masculinising male hormones results in a deepening of the voice, coarser features, facial hair, and the possibility of male pattern baldness. Surgery may involve the removal of breast tissue via a mastectomy, removal of female reproductive organs, and for those who choose it, the creation of a neo-phallus to mimic the physical appearance of a penis.

Many female to male (FTM) post-operative transsexuals have little problem 'passing' as males at first glance. The masculinising effects of the male hormones, together with the frequent decision to retain facial hair, leaves scarce evidence of the underlying former female biological sex. This is in contrast to the male to female post-operative transsexuals who often find that the addition of female hormones is not enough to mask the signs of masculinity, e.g. broad, coarse features, deep voice, and facial hair.

Whilst post-operatively, the genitalia of male to female transsexuals may be difficult to distinguish from that of a biological female at examination, this is not the case with FTM transsexuals. An artificially constructed phallus (phalloplasty) is made from either a tube of tissue re-distributed from the forearm area, or abdominal tissue, or (rarely) from back tissue. While the tissue is organised into a tube to physically mimic the appearance of a penis, some find that the end result lacks a convincing relationship to an actual penis although surgical techniques are being improved all the time. The tissue has no erectile function but some may opt to have a bendable stiffening insert or have a pump placed in the artificially created scrotum, whereby the neo-phallus may be manually inflated in order to erect. Due to the limitations of FTM genital surgery, in terms of appearance and functionality, many FTM transsexuals opt not to have phalloplasty. The masculinising hormones enlarges the clitoris, which is satisfactory for many FTM transsexuals.

Andrew Ives, a leading surgeon in gender reassignment surgery in Australia has provided a detailed account of both male-to-female and female-to-male surgical procedures and illustrations in chapter 14 of this book.

SECTION 2

UNDERSTANDING GENDER DYSPHORIA

CHAPTER 6

A BRIEF HISTORY OF GENDER DYSPHORIA

EARLY THEORISTS

Transsexualism first hit the headlines when the first sex-change operations were being performed in the 1960s. Around this time, psychoanalysis still had a strong presence in the fields of psychiatry and psychology. This was before the development of theoretical frameworks to help us understand mental processes and the rise of biological psychiatry, with its focus on the brain and pharmaceutical interventions. During the 1960s and 1970s, the most prominent psychiatrist and psychoanalyst writing about transsexualism was the American Robert Stoller, whose books included 'Sex and Gender' and 'The Transsexual Experiment'. Stoller conducted a number of studies of adult transsexual patients, and studies of children who appeared to have the early signs of gender identity disorder, and also examined their parents.

Stoller came up with his own hypothesis as to why some biological males developed into adult transsexuals. He described a mother who, typically, was depressed and relatively asexual in her own gender presentation, and in a relationship with the emotionally distant father of the child. He suggested that this mother would give birth to a beautiful baby boy who would bring a spark to her life, and said it would be the start of a close, enmeshed relationship between them. He described the closeness between the mother and son as far closer than would normally be expected – to the extent that the father was virtually out of the picture. The mother and son would be an inseparable duo. Stoller suggested that, as a result, the boy would grow up almost as an appendage to his mother, and fail to develop a separate male identity of his own. He went further to suggest that the boy's close identification with his mother resulted in the absence of any castration anxiety, as manifested by some adult transsexuals who seek castration and removal of their male genitalia.

While Stoller's postulated hypothesis may offer some plausibility to those uninitiated in the field, it is certainly not an accurate *'one-description fits all'* for all adults with gender dysphoria. The limitation of Stoller's work was that along with much of psychoanalysis, grand sweeping theories are extrapolated from the study of a very small number of cases. These are taken to be representative of a category of people who are presumed to be all the same, without any variation. Having worked in a specialist child and adolescent gender identity service, I have certainly seen young boys presenting to services, whose relationship with their mother and father definitely fit into Stoller's description, but it is by no means universal. For every person who neatly fits into the Stollerian template of the male to female transsexual, there are several others who do not. What is clear is that gender dysphoria covers a wide variety of people who arrive at a similar point (the wish to change gender) but the means by which they get there may be widely diverse. The obvious point to make is that Stoller's observations and extrapolated ideas were only made in relation to trans females. He did not offer any descriptions or ideas in relation to trans males.

Around the same time as Stoller, the American psychologist John Money was writing his own seminal work in the field. The 1970s saw the beginning of the ascent of biological psychiatry to the position it has today. John Money was the main figure in the nature vs. nurture debate regarding gender identity. He was a New Zealand-born psychologist and sexologist who spent much of his career working at the Sex Behaviour Unit at John Hopkins University. He famously wrote about the case of one of his patients, David Reimer, whom he referred to as the 'John / Joan' case in his book 'Man & Woman, Boy & Girl', which has continued to receive media attention and controversy to this day. David Reimer, who was one of two twin boys, suffered a catastrophic surgical accident during a routine circumcision in his first year of life, resulting in the loss of most of his penis. John Money recommended that David's sex be reassigned to female.

At the age of two, a further operation was performed to remove David's testes and create an artificial neo-vagina, and he received hormones later in childhood. John Money's hypothesis was that if David was not told of his biological sex through childhood and adolescence, and he was raised as a girl, then his gender identity would become female through environmental nurture.

Money published several papers and books reporting the experiment to have been a success and that David ('John') had successfully been raised as 'Joan'. However, some decades later it emerged that the endeavour had actually failed badly. David had reverted to his male gender as a teenager, and both he and his twin brother were suffering considerable mental health problems. Tragically, both David and his twin committed suicide in their mid-30s. At this point, there was renewed media interest in the story, which had been reported as a complete turnaround, and a triumph of nature over nurture. Much was made of the failure of the attempt to nurture an imposed gender identity different to the biological sex.

Amidst all the original and subsequent reporting of the David Reimer account, there has been one important psychological oversight ...

Little or indeed no reference has been made to the potentially pivotal role of secret knowledge of the experiment within the family context. The experiment was to determine whether a biological boy could have been successfully raised as a girl in order to develop a female gender identity, without the boy ever knowing he was born a boy. The flaw in this unfortunate experiment was that, of course, his parents, who continued to raise him, knew the secret of David's real sex. Whilst the parents may not have revealed their secret, we should not underestimate the role of unspoken communication within close–knit groups such as the family. David may not have officially known or even have been told, but the fact that both his parents, and the doctors, and psychologists all knew he was a biological male is, potentially, critically important in terms of the power of unspoken, unintentional (and in psychoanalytic language, *unconscious*) communication. The role that such communication had with David and his emerging sense of gender identity will of course never be known. However, the experiment could never have been regarded as definitive proof or failure of the nature vs. nurture debate as it was critically flawed with regard to this otherwise overlooked aspect of unspoken communication within families.

Milton Diamond is a sexologist and Professor of Anatomy and Reproductive Biology at the University of Hawaii and the Director of the Pacific Centre for Sex and Society. Diamond has published extensively in the area of sex, gender, sexuality, intersex, and transgender since the early 1960s. Those of us who have met him have observed his great passion and enthusiasm for the field in which he has become one of the leading authorities. His work examines the interplay of biological with environmental factors in the development of sexual and gender identities. His much-referenced quote is that *'Nature loves diversity, society hates it'*. Milton Diamond has always been a critic of John Money's proposed findings from the John / Joan case.

Diamond proposes that factors prior to birth, including genes and hormones, are instrumental in the development of gender identity. He suggests that gender identity is not neutral at the time of birth, but strongly influenced by biological sex, although greatly modifiable by subsequent environmental experiences. He discounts the suggestions of 'imprinting' or 'learning theory' as a basis for gender role acquisition, but rather considers it to be a composite of influences before and after birth. What he has proposed is a theory of gender development where genetics and hormones act as *'organising factors'* prior to birth, and subsequently impact on behaviours such as attitude and temperament after birth. He describes the 'organising factors' undergoing an *'activation process'* in response to social or environmental influences such as life events, stressors or puberty. It is through this sex-related *'activation process'* that the person comes to identify as male or female with their gender. Diamond describes a 'biased interaction' theory, whereby the prenatal *'organizing forces'* influence or bias the person's response to environmental or social forces. Through comparisons the person makes between themselves and their peers, they come to identify with individuals they are like, and individuals they are unlike, categorising themselves as *'same'* or *'different'*, especially in relation to sex and gender. Diamond has referred to *'brain sex'* or people having a *'gendered brain'*, based on the assumption that it is the brain which forms the basis of the personality, primarily from inherent prenatal tendencies which then interact with post-birth experiences.

FINDINGS FROM MY OWN WORK
WITH GENDER DYSPHORIA

Working in the fields of plastic surgery and then psychiatry and psychotherapy has exposed me to the differing relationships and understanding of gender dysphoria from each of these health professional groups. The surgeons who are master craftsmen of their trade understandably focus on the physical reconstructive aspects of the bodywork, and outsource any consideration of the transgender person's mind to other professionals. General psychiatrists, in the main, also avoid having to think about their patients' gender confusion by outsourcing the gender-dysphoric patients to specialist gender identity clinics. The psychiatrists in the gender identity clinics diagnose the presence of a gender dysphoria and if the patient is considered an appropriate candidate for sex reassignment, the focus will return to the body and the administration of hormones and surgery. As such, these psychiatrists are frequently perceived by the gender patients not as psychiatrists but as *gatekeepers* to the surgeons. The gender clinic psychiatrists will also consider whether there are co-existing psychiatric disorders which may be impacting on the gender identity problem. But any in-depth analytic exploration or psychotherapy with the patient may be outsourced to a psychotherapist if such a specialist resource is available.

Physical treatments of hormones and surgery may help people presenting with fixed 'transgender' identities corresponding to the opposite sex. But relatively permanent physical solutions are less appropriate for people presenting with less fixed, less binary, more fluid gender identities. Such gender presentations may vary over time or won't fit neatly into a male / female binary framework, and others may decide that they do not wish to pursue gender transition and role change in their everyday lives. For these people, a specially adapted form of specialist psychotherapy may be a more helpful intervention.

One of the problems with psychotherapy and counselling is the limited availability of professionals with appropriate training. What does exist may differ greatly in terms of what it consists of, and what its aims are. The majority of psychological interventions are surprisingly not aimed at working with the patient to try and help them to understand their sense of confusion or unhappiness in relation to their gender dysphoria. Instead, much intervention is aimed at helping people to either fit into a gender role or support them through a physical gender transition. Such therapies would be of little or no use to those people who are not considering gender transition or with non-binary gender presentations. Only a few writers over recent years have written papers attempting to understand gender identity disorders or transgender. Many of us who do are often met with criticism by those who do not consider it necessary for psychiatrists and psychotherapists to attempt to understand the condition, and who assert that physical bodily interventions should be offered.

Whilst working within a psychotherapeutic environment it became apparent to me that there was a split within the profession with regards to gender dysphoria. There were very traditional psychoanalytic psychotherapists who usually had little or no clinical experience of people with gender dysphoria but who nevertheless held firm, almost religious, beliefs and convictions based on speculations which made sense to them. They held the view that gender dysphoria was either a psychosis (characterised by delusions) or a perversion whose function was to defend against a psychosis, which would threaten to disintegrate mental functioning. This was the view of many of my professional colleagues within the clinic in which I was working at the time. The other stance taken by much of psychiatry was seemingly not to think about it much at all, and for the focus to stay on patients' bodies, without much in the way of interventions aimed at the inner workings of their minds.

So there appeared to be a very polarised split between the health professionals in relation to gender dysphoria. The clinicians who focussed on physical treatments of hormones and surgery were perceived as being *'for'* gender dysphoria and sex reassignment. Those who believed it was a psychosis were, at times, perceived to be *'against'* the condition. These perceptions were perpetuated by some members of the transgender community and also extended to the professionals themselves, who saw each other as occupying the opposite side in an uncomfortable, and occasionally adversarial, divide. In my paper 'Parallel Processes', I suggested that such a perceived 'for' and 'against' split within the profession directly mirrored the binary male / female split, which was central to the gender conflict for those with gender dysphoria. I suggested that this apparent professional split wasn't mere coincidence, but genuinely relevant in the way it showed the gender dysphoric situation extending into the professional arena.

Neither of these positions offered any clinical value to my patients with gender dysphoria. The specially adapted psychotherapy service I set up in 2001 had, as a main constituent, a group-based therapy component which functioned as a weekly thinking and working group of patients and therapist collaborating together. As such, it doesn't involve a therapist speculating hypotheses in isolation, but collaboratively with the gender dysphoric patients themselves. The thinking occurs weekly and the patients attend for several months or a few years. This role as a psychiatrist working in a psychotherapeutic role within a specially adapted psychological service, serving a variety of gender-related conditions, has informed my understanding of transgender, and is the basis of much of this book.

CHAPTER 7

THE ONSET AND EVOLUTION
OF GENDER DYSPHORIA

The first and most important thing to do when a person is referred to a professional for gender dysphoria is to carry out a thorough assessment. It is essential that the assessment should include a detailed history of the person's life from birth to the present day. Amongst the events and developmental stages of life we need to discover what it was like to be that person at those various stages of their life. How was it for them being a child? How did they relate to their parents and friends? We need to get an insider's perspective on what is was like for them, emotionally and psychologically, growing up and developing through their formative experiences.

What was noticeable early in my specialist psychotherapy service was that there appeared to be two types of history being given by my patients: the 'official' one and the 'real' one. The 'official' one had been prepared and rehearsed in accordance with what the patient envisaged the assessor 'needed to hear'. I became alert to this once I had heard several patients give an almost identical account, which sounded rehearsed, with little emotion and lacking personalised detail. These stories resembled those found in the biographies of famous transsexuals (that many of us will have read) where the biological male describes 'never fitting in with the other boys' or liking 'rough and tumble play' and wanting to 'spend time with the girls,' having 'always thought of themselves as a little girl'. These patients had done their homework; their internet research had informed them that psychiatrists needed to be satisfied that their patients had certain characteristics or histories in order for them to progress past the psychiatrist, (who is generally portrayed as the *'gatekeeper'* between the transgender patient and gender reassignment).

Unlike the psychiatrists working in gender clinics offering hormones and surgery, I was a psychiatrist offering psychotherapy alone, so, not a gatekeeper! Whenever it became apparent that a patient was delivering a rehearsed 'official' version of events, I would interrupt them mid-way through their telling of the life they were purporting to have had, and reassured them whatever they told me would be in confidence; it would not jeopardise any treatments they were receiving from any (gate-keeping) gender clinicians they were also consulting. This generally inspired a great sense of relief, and then they'd tell me the accurate version of their personal history. This kind of scenario was a very frequent occurrence.

So how were the 'real' histories, which the patients eventually offered, different?

The primary difference was the onset of the gender dysphoria or change in gender identity. Rather than this arising 'from birth' as the patients often attempted to convey initially, most later admitted that there was an initial period of time where the gender identity usually corresponded with the biological sex, prior to the onset of a change in gender identity. The common sequence of events, as described by many gender identity patients in the psychotherapy service, is shown overleaf in Diagram 1. I have divided the evolution of a gender dysphoria into eight stages, which I will deal with in turn.

Diagram 1: *Reported sequence of gender identity change.*

1 Potential vulnerability factors pre / post birth

2 Initial gender identity congruent with biological sex

3 An early sign or symptom of 'something not quite right' + / - change in mood – known as a prodrome period

4 Period of searching for meaning behind the experienced change in self

5 Experienced change in self attributed to gender identity

6 Increasing preoccupation with sense of gender identity, and realisation that a change of perception to gender identity is needed to address experienced changes

7 Retrospective attribution of gender as cause of problems in various areas of life to date

8 Heightened awareness of gender in everyday life in relation to self and others

The point of time at which the sense of gender identity was different for each individual, but was usually preceded by a period of time where there were other noticeable changes experienced by the person. This pivotal period prior to the change in gender identity may have included a period of general confusion about other aspects of their identity, a noticeable change in their prevailing mood or day-to-day functioning, and the commonly reported sense of 'something not feeling quite right' (Stage (3) in Diagram 1). In psychiatry, 'delusional mood' is sometimes used as the technical term for *a sense of something not feeling quite right,*' but the use of the term delusional in this context is completely distinct from the usual use of the term and should not be confused in this regard. Whether or not the reported sense of 'something not being quite right' is a precursor to the change in gender identity, is debateable, but the important observation is the sequence of events as shown in Diagram 1.

The initial period of gender identity corresponding with the biological sex varies. If the above model is universal, this period may have been so short as to not be remembered in people who claim to have always had a 'transgender' identity. However, in the majority of patients with gender presentations, the above sequence has been recounted with the onset of a change in gender identity occurring at a later stage, anywhere from early childhood to late adulthood. There is sometimes the fear that one may not be considered a real or true transsexual unless one has always (or professed to have always) had a transgender identity or that they may be less legitimately transgender if one experienced a gender identity corresponding with their biological sex beforehand. These notions are of course false. So every trans person should be reassured of this. There are many very real and very legitimate trans people who openly admit to living happily in their biological gender for a period of time prior to the onset of vulnerability factors.

POTENTIAL VULNERABILITY FACTORS BEFORE OR AFTER BIRTH

I have incorporated this into the sequential trajectory as there appeared to be a number of common factors described by my patients, which may have played a contributory role in the development of their own particular gender dysphoria. The emphasis here is that these factors appeared to be significant because they were reported by several people, although by no means universally. This suggests that the presence of such factors may potentially be relevant and warrant consideration in understanding the evolution of a particular person's gender dysphoria whilst being less relevant to the evolution of the gender dysphoria in someone else. Vulnerability factors may be biological, such as genetic factors determined before birth or injury, trauma or brain infection acquired post birth. However, none of these factors were the subject of my investigation, which concentrated on reported life events in their personal histories. The factors, which were more commonly reported, are listed in Table 2.

Table 2: *Potential vulnerability factors relevant to gender dysphoria.*

Replacement baby (following previous loss of child / stillborn child of opposite sex)
Initial period of cross-sex rearing

The factor described as 'replacement baby' refers to people who were conceived soon after the loss of an older sibling through childhood death, or a stillborn baby, or termination of pregnancy. The conception may have been planned as a way for the parents to deal with the emotional loss of the previous child or the end of a pregnancy – involving a child of the opposite sex in both cases. People who report this as a feature of their early life sometimes report the sense that they never believed that they *'lived up to'* their parents' expectations of their idealised lost older sibling, even if they were never overtly told this by their parents.

There is a small number of people with gender dysphoria who describe an overtly gender-confused upbringing, where a parent or caregiver would have preferred to have had a child of the opposite sex, and so decided to raise the child from birth in the opposite gender role for a period of time. Some have described this having occurred for a few years, while more extreme cases described this cross-gender rearing going on until close to puberty, which, understandably, caused much confusion in their developing gender identity. Such cases are, of course, relatively rare.

Another factor observed in common with many people I assess with gender dysphoria is the preference for logical thinking, combined with a higher than usual ability in mathematics, physics and computer / software programming. Such a logical way of thinking with a preponderance to understanding concepts in a binary (black / white, right / wrong, on / off) manner can be a feature of Asperger Syndrome, which lies on the autistic spectrum. Some of the people exhibiting such thinking styles may have received a formal diagnosis of Asperger's. Some may fulfil the diagnostic criteria, but have never been formally diagnosed, and others may merely have Asperger's traits. The more logical brain prefers definite categories over fluid uncertainty, and the preference to consider life in an 'either / or' binary system lends itself to a 'male / female' trans binary, rather than a more gender subversive or gender fluid position.

In my opinion, a great deal of gender dysphoria patients I have assessed with very rigid convictions regarding their need to pursue gender reassignment have features suggestive of Asperger Syndrome. This is less so in those presenting with atypical presentations which make them less rigid and more fluid in terms of their gender identity, or presenting with autogynaephilia, or confused as to whether they are transgender or transvestite.

Of course, none of these 'vulnerability factors' alone are enough to create gender dysphoria in a person. They may serve as a potential foundation upon which a gender dysphoria may develop, with the addition of subsequent factors. These subsequent instrumental factors may be biological, psychological, or social, or a combination of these.

1) Initial gender identity congruent with biological sex

As mentioned earlier, it is common for many of my patients to initially give an 'official' history of their life wherein they had always held a gender identity corresponding to the opposite sex. But once they're reassured that I am not a 'gatekeeper' a more accurate and individualised personal history is obtained. What I hear then is that, following birth and during early development, there is usually a period of gender-identity corresponding to their biological sex. This lasts for a varying duration before the next phase, as described below, takes place.

2) Prodrome period of 'something not quite right' + / - change in mood

After a period of gender-identity corresponding with their biological sex spanning any number of years there appears to be an event which results in a marked change in their psychological functioning. This appears to happen at any age, and I have had patients describing it happening in early childhood, late childhood, adolescence, early / middle / late adulthood. What they describe is a time-limited period during which there is a reduction in everyday functioning. The description given often resembles what we would consider as a period of depression or what many people would refer to as a 'breakdown' of some form, but as it is only described in retrospective terms and not observed clinically first hand, it is difficult to know what this may be or what may cause it. There is a variety of possible explanations, including functional psychological conditions such as an episode of depression, or biological causes such as a gene-activated condition, or any number of phenomena occurring within the brain, but we could only speculate if any of them were accurate. I will allow someone else the exciting challenge of looking into this further!

Once this time-limited period of reduced functioning is over, there is a reported recovery of sorts, almost like a re-booting, but with the person describing a residual sense of something not quite feeling right within themselves and how they perceive themselves. The sense of reported disturbance is often difficult for the person to accurately describe, other than knowing that 'something was not right' having otherwise fully recovered from the preceding period of feeling more out of sorts. This is most probably the beginning of the onset of the 'dysphoria' before it becomes more firmly experienced specifically as a 'gender dysphoria'.

3) Period of searching for meaning behind the experienced change in self

Once someone finds himself or herself with a persisting sense of 'something not being quite right' there understandably follows a period of time where they search for what the underlying reason is for the dysphoria they're experiencing so they can address it and return to optimal functioning.

4) Experienced change in self-attributed to gender identity

After a period of searching, the person understands their experienced feeling of dysphoria rests within the framework of gender, and that the dysphoria must be in relation to their own sense of gender-identity. Correspondingly, the understanding arises that if their sex / gender may be addressed on a physical level then the experience of 'something not being quite right' will also be addressed.

5) Increasing preoccupation with sense of gender identity and realisation that change to gender identity is needed to address experienced changes

The realisation that gender is at the root of the experienced dysphoria, the decision to address the problem by changing their gender is reported by many as bringing relief to the preceding period of relative uncertainty. This 'working through' is not revisited psychologically, irrespective of how early on this understanding is reached (early childhood in some, and later as an adult in others). Rather than re-visit and re-examine the preceding steps, the subsequent mental efforts are directed and focussed on addressing what is now understood to be the solution for the gender dysphoria, i.e. steps towards changing gender.

6) Retrospective attribution of gender as cause of problems in various areas of life to date

The preceding stages then appear to be followed by the person looking back over their life to date and considering whether 'gender' could have explained other aspects of their life so far. As humans, we are prone to retrospectively attribute meaning once we have come to an understanding at a later date. We are prone to looking back selectively, highlighting relevant past data which corresponds to our current hypothesis or our understanding of a situation. We refer to this as 'retrospective bias' and 'attribution error'. This is no different with gender dysphoria where more credibility or relevance may be given to aspects of our past which may similarly have occurred in the early lives of someone without a gender dysphoria, but as such, does not have such a retrospective significance. For example, my teenage niece is an amazing footballer, but she does not have any gender dysphoria. As a child, I enjoyed playing with dolls, I loathed playing rugby at school, and, as an adolescent, during the post-punk goth era, I wore quite a bit of eyeliner and lipstick, but I did not have a gender dysphoria. For the person with a gender dysphoria, memories of attributes not corresponding with gender stereotypes not only serve as reinforcing evidence of the perceived gender dysphoria but also suggest that the gender dysphoria 'may always have been there'. What may be more accurate is that behaviour not fitting in with gender stereotypes may have already existed in the person prior to the onset of their gender dysphoria. But once the gender dysphoria was known to be present, such data is retrospectively given more importance, and leads us to believe that the gender dysphoria must have 'always existed, ever since I can remember'.

7) Heightened awareness of gender in everyday life in relation to self and others

Once the gender dysphoria is established, there may be a subsequent weighting afforded to gender-related data, and a heightened awareness of gender on a day-to-day basis, to a degree that other bio-socio-demographic variables are not experienced as prominently, e.g. race, ethnicity, social class, height, weight or other factors.

The observed sequence of events is just that, it is not an attempt at explaining causality.

The sequence of events we've described above is merely the path the gender dysphoria has developed in the vast majority of people I have assessed, through in-depth personal interviews. Although there is a recognised sequential set of stages, it does not imply any particular cause for the gender dysphoria. I have no idea as to how gender dysphoria arises, and others whose professional lives are devoted to researching this are better placed to advise on this. For every proponent of a psychological cause, there will be a proponent of a biological cause. Within those who suggest a biological cause, these will be further sub-divided into those who suggest the cause was determined pre-birth, and those who suggest the cause was biological, but post-birth. The sequence of events described in this book is merely that: an observed sequence without any implication for underlying cause. As with many conditions, I suspect the cause may well be multifactorial and more complicated than a binary (nature / nurture) one. I also suspect that the reasons or causes may indeed be different for different people with different presentations of gender dysphoria. Whilst the presenting condition of something not being right about gender and wanting to change it may sound similar, the route by which it was arrived at may differ vastly.

CHAPTER 8

PSYCHOTHERAPY FOR GENDER DYSPHORIA

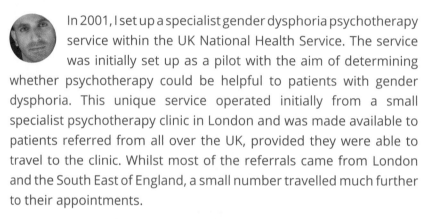 In 2001, I set up a specialist gender dysphoria psychotherapy service within the UK National Health Service. The service was initially set up as a pilot with the aim of determining whether psychotherapy could be helpful to patients with gender dysphoria. This unique service operated initially from a small specialist psychotherapy clinic in London and was made available to patients referred from all over the UK, provided they were able to travel to the clinic. Whilst most of the referrals came from London and the South East of England, a small number travelled much further to their appointments.

The usual reason for people being referred to the service was a feeling of unhappiness or confusion with their sense of gender identity that they hoped a talking therapy might resolve. If the gender disturbance was part of a transgender identity the patients may also have been referred to a gender clinic (or I would have referred them) so they could be assessed for physical treatments, such as hormones and sex reassignment surgery. The two services were independent of each other, but certainly not mutually exclusive. There are advantages and disadvantages to being situated separately from a gender clinic offering physical treatments.

The advantage is that patients have the reassurance of knowing that whatever they discuss in their therapy assessment or sessions will have no influence on whether they are granted hormones or surgery. This is especially important, given that, as we have mentioned, patients commonly perceive the doctors at gender clinics as 'gatekeepers' between them and the procedures they believe they want. They know they can discuss any ambivalence or doubts about prospective physical gender interventions honestly, without feeling like they're in danger of jeopardising a pathway of physical treatment. As I only offered the patients in my gender dysphoria service psychotherapy and nothing else, they know that they don't need to convince me of anything or jump through any hoops en route to a sex change.

The disadvantage is the risk of what is referred to in mental health as 'splitting' between services which are played off each other, sometimes in a paranoid or hostile manner, usually because of a lack of adequate communication. This can lead to uncorrected presumptions about one service by the other or by patients. Ultimately, clinicians in both services are working towards the same goal, which is to best serve the needs of the gender dysphoric persons referred to them, in a manner, which will provide results that offer lasting satisfaction. Adequate communication between the physically and operationally distinct services usually satisfactorily address any inter-service splits, which become apparent from time to time.

Before the gender dysphoria psychotherapy service was set up, it was unclear whether people with gender dysphoria would be interested in psychotherapy, whether they would persist with it or find it useful, and to what extent we'd need to adapt usual therapeutic delivery and technique to make it work. Colleagues had suggested that patients with gender dysphoria would not be interested in psychotherapy. Some people even suggested that people with gender identity conditions should not be offered psychotherapy or any other psychological interventions, and should only be offered physical interventions aimed at their bodies. This seemed to me to discriminate against people with gender dysphoria, who deserved the opportunity to access a psychological talking therapy, which may be in a dedicated specialist service (as with therapy services for other distinct groups, e.g. women's services, or those specifically for black and ethnic minority groups). We found that those with gender dysphoria who were offered psychotherapy consistently stayed with the intervention. They reported that it improved the stability of, and their satisfaction with, their sense of gender identity, whether that is their primary biological one, a transgender identity, or indeed a non-binary gender identity (when the individual chooses not to identify as male, female or transgender).

AIMS OF THE THERAPEUTIC TREATMENT

The aims of the therapy are psychological rather than physical. The therapy takes place irrespective of any physical changes which the person may be undergoing or planning to undergo. The therapy has two explicit goals. The first is to attempt to understand the extent to which the person may be preoccupied with gender as a construct in their daily lives, and work towards them feeling less persecuted, troubled, or aware of gender and any associated distress. At the same time, we'll work towards helping the person to develop a greater understanding of the meaning they afford to gender as a construct in relation to themselves and society. The second aim is to enable the person to attain a stability, acceptance, and satisfaction with their individually tailored gender role, which may or may not correlate with their biological sex, and may or may not fit within a binary male / female framework of gender. Reducing the extent by which the person is preoccupied by gender-related matters, and achieving a greater sense of stability and security in their sense of their own gender (irrespective of their own biological sex) will help them, regardless of whether they choose surgical alteration of their physical sex.

The aim of the therapy is not to help people transition through a sex change, and nor is it to try to persuade them against having a sex change. Neither of these aims is appropriate as they would indicate an overt or hidden agenda on the part of the therapist, who would not be in a position to help the patient, as their own political, moral or religious ideals would interfere with their ability to adopt an essentially impartial position. I would go as far as to suggest that a clinician who has strong political, moral or other reasons for believing that all people with gender dysphoria should be given gender reassignment, or conversely, that none be allowed to access gender reassignment, is not in a position to offer psychotherapy to this patient group.

The aims for each individual person are individually tailored to that individual and mutually agreed between patient and therapist during the initial assessment.

ASSESSMENT

I wanted my therapy service to be available to as many people as possible, or at least, to exclude as few as possible. As such, I limited the exclusion criteria to those persons who had an active drug or alcohol dependence, or a clinically obvious psychosis (which we call a frank psychosis) as their ability to use the therapy would have been compromised. For these individuals, I would offer a limited number of individual consultations rather than the group programme.

When the referral comes in from their health care provider, we would invite the patient in for one or two hour-long assessments. The assessment consists of taking a detailed account of what the person is seeking professional help for, and then talking through a detailed history of their life to date, giving attention to biological sex, and gender identity development in addition to their sexual and relationship history. This is essential in order to discern whether the presenting gender-related symptom is solely located in gender identity, or is linked primarily to sexual interests or feelings that cause the patient distress.

Table 3: Conditions relating to sexual interest with an apparent gender identity presentation.

Transvestism: Interest in the outer appearance / clothing of the opposite sex

Fetishistic transvestism: Sexual excitation in clothes of the opposite sex

Autogynaephilia: Sexual fantasy of having female body parts as a man

Homosexuality / lesbianism: Confusion regarding sense of gender can result from attraction to members of the same sex, which the patient feels is unacceptable

A breakdown of the first 82 people assessed and / or treated by the service is indicated in Table 4 below:

Table 4: *Types of conditions involving people referred to the gender dysphoria psychotherapy service.*

Pre-operative transsexual: 61%	
Post-operative transsexual: 26%	
Dual role transvestism: 13%	
Fetishistic transvestism: 15%	
Autogynaephilia: 5%	
Proportion of female to male: (FTM) 17%	
(patients may have more than one condition at once)	

The above table indicates that almost two thirds of the people in the service considered themselves to be pre-operative transsexuals. A quarter of the people referred were post-operative transsexuals with a persisting sense of dissatisfaction or gender dysphoria, even after physical sex-reassignment. Just over a quarter of people were referred as having a gender identity condition but, after assessment, were considered to be transvestites rather than having a gender dysphoria. The ratio of biological males to females referred to the service was approximately six to one. It is of course important to remember that these are the proportions relating to the population of persons referred to a specialist gender dysphoria psychotherapy service, and not representative of the proportions of these categories of people in the general public, or who attend other gender services or clinics.

When taking a clinical history, careful attention needs to be paid to the person's understanding of their sense of gender identity spanning from early childhood to the present, including any periods when the sense of gender identity was concordant with their biological sex. It is not uncommon for a person with gender dysphoria to initially attempt to provide what I have referred to previously as 'the official version' of their life history, almost a 'cut and paste' approach in accordance with what they anticipate professionals in gender clinics need to hear in order for them to access to physical treatments. If someone does provide such a generic template of a history, then reassurance on the part of the assessor may encourage them to give a more accurate account.

THERAPEUTIC MODEL AND DELIVERY

Following assessment, the person is offered a few individual consultations, the number will be tailored to their assessed needs. The main purpose of these sessions is to allow the person to establish a therapeutic relationship with the therapist before they join a weekly psychotherapy group for 75-minute sessions. The groups are classed as 'slow-open', having a set membership (up to eight) whose places are filled as members of the group are discharged. The overall length of treatment is determined by the patient and informed by their response to, and benefit from, the therapy. Most patients in the service find that the difficulties they present relating to their sense of gender identity are satisfactorily addressed within two years of weekly attendance.

The group sessions involve a modified group-analytic psychotherapy. Group-analytic therapy was devised by the psychiatrist S.H. Foulkes in the early 1970s and has its root in psychoanalysis, social theory, and systems theory. The therapy is delivered to all the members in the group by all the members of the group, not merely by the therapist alone. Rather than it being a room of patients waiting for the therapist to address each of their problems, it is a working group, in which everyone collaborates, and works together in order to help each other. In the specialist adaptation of the therapy for gender dysphoria, the group-analytic therapy was combined with another type of therapy called Mentalisation Based Therapy (MBT).

MBT was devised by Professors Bateman and Fonagy for use with patients with emotionally unstable personality disorder, not for gender dysphoria (see Table 4). Have delivered this type of therapy to patients with personality disorder for many years in a separate service which I ran alongside the NHS, I realised that an adaptation of MBT may be usefully applied to gender dysphoria patients in my gender dysphoria service, even in the absence of any concurrent personality disorder.

Table 5: Mentalisation.

> **Mentalisation is the ability to recognise and understand feelings, intentional states, and mental processes within ourselves, in others and interpersonal contexts.**

SPECIALIST ADAPTATION OF THERAPEUTIC TECHNIQUE

In gender dysphoria psychotherapy, mentalisation involves working collaboratively with the person towards a greater understanding and clarity of their reported feelings or convictions regarding their experience of gender. Most of the patients initially struggled to consider and articulate the meanings and attributes they, or others, associate with gender. There was a tendency for assumptions about gender to remain unchallenged and without critical analysis. Such a lack of questioning or critique of assumptions or hypotheses would be classed as 'non-mentalising' in MBT. This gender-focussed 'non-mentalisation' includes mentalisation as to how others may perceive or attribute meanings regarding the patient's gender, such as appearance, clothing, behaviour, hobbies, and other aspects of their everyday life. The binary nature of the gender conflict, along with the social nature of gender, make group therapy the preferred approach. In individual therapy, therapists can find themselves drawn into a protagonist / antagonist dynamic with the patient that is very much like the male / female binary framework at the core of their difficult experience.

Analytic therapy groups can be classified as either *'homogenous'* or *'heterogeneous'* depending on whether the presentations of patients in the groups are similar or different. As all the patients in the gender dysphoria groups have, or have had, an issue relating to their sense of gender identity, the groups would be considered to be homogenous. The rationale for running a homogenous group for people with gender dysphoria was to avoid the risk that the gender condition would be either under or over-attended to in a more mixed (heterogeneous) group. In a homogenous group, in which the condition is present in some manifestation in all its members, it can be considered without occupying a continual focus, or feel like the unspoken 'elephant in the room'.

As already indicated, the therapy group may include persons who wish to pursue gender reassignment in the future, those who have already had surgery, and those who feel transgender, but have no intention to have surgery. The service also caters for people who are not easily categorised within a pre-operative or post-operative framework. Some show diagnostic fluidity between the categories of transgender and transvestite. There are also rare cases of autogynaephilia in which the person may wish to retain a male gender identity but with female genitalia or other female physical parts. So, while at first sight, the group might appear to be homogenous, it may actually be considered heterogeneous upon closer consideration.

Earlier in this book I described how there is often much confusion amongst both patients and professionals regarding the terms 'sex' and 'gender'. It is probably easiest if the biological, phenotypic, and chromosomal sex differences of 'male' and 'female' are considered as having a biological (organic) basis, in contrast to the role meanings afforded to these sexes in the form of 'masculine' and 'feminine' genders, which may be considered as social constructs. Gender is a psychosocial virtual entity without location in a person's body. It solely exists in, and is perpetuated by, the society in which the person lives.

People referred with gender dysphoria frequently have a rigid, binary perception of gender. They may feel that they do not comfortably fit into this framework and therefore feel persecuted by it. This mismatch usually leads them to question the validity of their own gender, rather than question the validity of the perceived gender framework. In contrast, gender-confident individuals may comfortably play with, or creatively subvert, societal gender frameworks without experiencing any insecurity in their own sense of gender identity. Such mixing and matching of elements from across the perceived binary divide is seen in the recent phenomenon of the 'metrosexual' male and the female 'ladette'.

In psychotherapy for gender dysphoria, the clinician's task is to deconstruct the rigid gender frameworks perceived by the patient, so as to open up a range of what is possible for the individual in any given gender role. When a patient uses the terms '*masculine*' or '*feminine*' within the therapy session, their understanding of these terms should not be presumed. Rather, it would be clarified by enquiry from the fellow group members and therapist in a manner of collaborative exploration within a mentalisation-based framework. The aim is not to discourage the use of the gender terms, but instead to encourage a degree of enquiry as to what they mean to those using them (mentalisation), rather than presume a universally understood meaning (non-mentalisation).

Although people may refer to 'male', or 'female' clothes, attitudes, mannerisms, thinking-styles, and interests, it is the work of the therapy group (patients and therapist together) to 'de-gender' the things that patients have 'gendered' in their minds. Long-standing 'gendering' adds to identity confusion when individuals find themselves mismatched with the perceived gendered framework. If aspects of themselves are identified as qualities they had classified as 'male' or 'female', a gender conflict will be reinforced if these are incongruent with their biological sex.

As regards to clothing in particular, the therapist should maintain that, although the person or the society in which they live assign gender associations to particular items of clothing, these are merely societal constructions. Therefore, an interest in any particular garment does not impart a greater or lesser validity to any particular gender identity. Patients should be encouraged to wear to sessions whatever they would normally wear, and any gendered associations they may have given their clothes may then be considered within the enquiring arena of the therapeutic group.

Gradually, pre-existing terms and conditions of gender are deconstructed, with the therapeutic aim of reducing the primacy or importance afforded to gender in the same benign manner in which they consider other aspects of themselves; e.g. height, age, social class, race or ethnicity. The rationale behind this is that if the pre-existing heightened awareness of gender is lessened to the extent that it no longer occupies an over-riding focus, there will be an associated reduction in their gender-related dissatisfaction and perceived discomfort and dysphoria. In simple terms, the person feels less persecuted and less troubled by issues relating to gender in their everyday life.

As well as reducing the extent to which the person is troubled by gender, the other function of the therapy is to enable the person to carve out a bespoke understanding of their gender identity. A person may arrive with a narrow repertoire of gender options, frequently limited to stereotyped 'masculine' and 'feminine' roles and attributes. Through time in the group where ideas and assumptions of gender are explored and critiqued, the person will be able to expand their repertoire of gender options and come to a more individually tailored understanding of themselves, rather than having to assimilate themselves into an off-the-shelf identity which may not suit them. The forum of the exploratory group will consider numerous gender constructs, including differing interpretations of what it is to be 'male' or 'female' in addition to non-binary gender identities such as 'gender-neutral' and 'gender-queer' or 'trans'.

By the time a person leaves the group, the hope is for them to achieve an individually-tailored gender identity which makes sense to them, which may or may not fit within a binary gender framework, and which may or may not correspond to their biological sex. The hope is that as the gender identity is individually tailored to meet their needs it will hopefully prove to be more stable over time, rather than changing from one identity to another. The additional aim is for the person to be less preoccupied and troubled by gender in their everyday life. In summary, the hope is for the person to be happier and less troubled by gender and have a gender-identity which they feel suits them, and remains stable over time.

CHAPTER 9

PARALLEL PROCESSES: OBSERVATIONS FROM PSYCHOTHERAPEUTIC WORK WITH GENDER DYSPHORIA

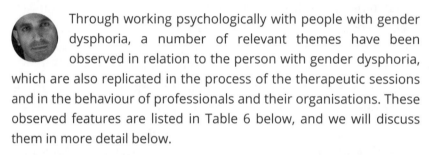 Through working psychologically with people with gender dysphoria, a number of relevant themes have been observed in relation to the person with gender dysphoria, which are also replicated in the process of the therapeutic sessions and in the behaviour of professionals and their organisations. These observed features are listed in Table 6 below, and we will discuss them in more detail below.

Table 6: Themes observed from psychological work with transgender people.

Confusion

Binary rigidity

Genital centrality

Questioning of authenticity

THEME 1: CONFUSION

Vignette: The therapy group are sent up from the waiting room, and as the familiar faces enter, an unfamiliar burly man with a gruff expression, wearing a baseball cap, accompanies them. Although I am the therapist to the group, I have no idea who this man is. My initial reaction is bewilderment, although I observe that none of the other group members seem to be bothered about the apparent infiltration of their group by this unknown man. I continue to observe, and, after what seems a very long

10 seconds I realize that the unknown man is Rose, who, after some weeks of talking about her frustration of feeling a fraud in her post-operative male to female identity, has now arrived as a 'man'. The group members had realised this in the waiting room, accounting for their lack of confusion.

Some of the members of the therapy group have rigid ideas in relation to gender at the time of referral to the service, but over time develop an increasing degree of fluidity (as well as confusion) in their understanding of their own and others' genders. Such confusion is not always confined to the members but may be displaced into the mind of their therapist as the above vignette illustrates. Therapists must be prepared for patients who present themselves in different gender roles, sometimes switching abruptly from one session to the next. It can be a challenge to face a familiar, yet unfamiliar patient.

The confusion can also extend to other parts of the institution: administrative and reception staff have to contend with changing gender pronouns, and management may be unsure which toilets patients should be allowed to use in the building. Some years ago, I was asked to assess a transgender person who was an inmate within a prison. The person was a biological male who had been started on female hormones and had developed breasts as a result. The prisoners were all required to have pat-down body searches upon returning from exercise, but this particular prisoner had been refusing to be handled by male staff in light of his developing *'female'* breasts. This caused some confusion and difficulty within the prison system; they wanted to respect the patient's wishes and dignity without compromising the security of the prison. The prison decided that the inmate should have a female prison officer conduct the pat-down search of the inmate's upper body, and have male prison officers conduct the pat-down search from the waist down.

THEME 2: BINARY RIGIDITY

Vignette: Once again, we return to the earlier vignette where Rose arrives at the group therapy session as a man. Further into the session, Rose talked of how her original motivation for gender reassignment was to remedy not 'feeling right' as a man, but that post-transition, she had 'not felt right' as a woman either, and so had wondered about going back to being 'male' again. The group members suggested that, rather than oscillating from one gender to another, she should spend some time in the group working out what it was that 'did not feel right' in herself and why she had linked this to her sense of gender identity. The group members suggested that such a psychological enquiry may be more useful for Rose than assimilating herself into one or more binary gender 'solutions'.

A rigid adherence to a binary system of gender rules could be considered as fundamental to gender dysphoria. It is common for people to give a history of 'not feeling right' early in the evolution of their gender dysphoria process. The mismatch between their interests and characteristics, and what they perceive society dictates as being 'appropriate' to their biological sex serves as confirmation to them of their gender dysphoria. A similar 'not feeling right' is sometimes reported by the people referred for therapy, for whom sex-reassignment surgery did not provide the psychological solution they had hoped for and who once again find themselves in a body that they felt to be wrong for them. We will return to this later in the book.

As illustrated in the vignettes, during therapy it is common for people to abruptly switch to a particular gender presentation, and just as abruptly, switch back in a subsequent session. It is just as common for a post-operative transgender patient to return suddenly to the gender presentation of their original biological sex, or to oscillate between these two binary gender presentations. Such abrupt switching is more often observed at the early stages of therapy, perhaps as the patient acclimatises to the process of creative gender enquiry. This is an example of exploration occurring on a physical level before it moves to the psychological one. Switching between binary gender 'solutions' must be tolerated by the therapist, and enquiries into its meaning should be considered collaboratively with the patient by the rest of the therapy group.

Binary rigidity is not solely confined to the person with the gender dysphoria. Within the clinical setting, professionals often find themselves either drawn into occupying (or are misperceived as occupying) binary stances on a number of politically charged topics in relation to gender identity. Most commonly, professionals are perceived, accurately or inaccurately, as adopting either *'for'* or *'against'* positions in relation to sex-reassignment surgery. Not only individuals, but entire institutions come to be perceived, sometimes completely unjustly, as rigidly adopting such binary stances. For some years, the specialist gender dysphoria psychotherapy service at the clinic was presumed by many to be *'transphobic'* for offering psychotherapy rather than physical (hormonal / surgical) treatment. This is at odds with the experience of the patients within the service, many of whom were in receipt of psychotherapeutic *and* physical interventions concurrently from respective clinics, and benefited from both. I would advise clinicians entering this field to be wary of, and to avoid being drawn into, such binary positions with regards to transgender politics. I am of the firm opinion that maintaining an open mind and a position of neutrality, in combination with scientific curiosity and enquiry regarding the difficulty being presented, is a clinician's duty to their patient with gender dysphoria.

THEME 3: GENITAL CENTRALITY

> **Vignette:** Celia is a biological male whose long-standing preoccupation has been that he would be happier in life if he had a neo-vagina surgically created via a vaginoplasty operation.

For many people seeking professional help for gender dysphoria, the presenting problem is that their 'genitalia is wrong', rather than a sense of dissatisfaction, confusion or particular emotional response in relation to their genitalia. Many people with gender dysphoria referred to the service are clear in their minds that the primary problem is located in the sex of their body, and that the psychological problems they report are secondary to this, rather than vice versa.

However, such genital centrality is not restricted to the person with gender dysphoria and can at times be observed as a feature of the professionals and institutions involved in their care.

In the above vignette, the clinic's arbitrary classifying of patients on the basis of whether or not they had had sex reassignment surgery mirrored the genital centrality observed in some of the patients themselves.

> **Vignette:** Psychotherapists frequently ask whether people with gender dysphoria who appear focussed on physical genital solutions (hormones and surgery) should be offered psychotherapy at all. Numerous colleagues have even suggested that 'nothing can be done for post-operative transsexuals' who were dissatisfied after genital surgery.

Of course there is no evidence to support the suggested idea that intact genitals are required to receive benefit from psychotherapeutic interventions. The unfounded concerns appear to mirror the over-riding focus and preoccupation on genitalia which may be a feature, at times, with some people with gender dysphoria.

THEME 4: QUESTIONING OF AUTHENTICITY

A commonly reported feature is concern regarding the authenticity of gender role. People presenting with a sense of confusion or unhappiness (dysphoria) with their biological sex frequently describe *'not living up to'* what they believed was expected of them in the corresponding gender role. In their early years, this questioning of the authenticity of their gender role may initially have been by other people, but they would have later taken it on themselves. Unsurprisingly, a rigid adherence to perceived binary gender roles with which the individual feels mismatched, is often a precursor. Subsequently, they question whether they could, or should be, 'authentically' considered a member of the sex corresponding to their gender role or, indeed, whether a greater sense of legitimacy could be achieved by changing their gender role.

Physical sex reassignment provides a lasting solution to a mismatched gender identity for many transgender people. However, it is certainly not a universal solution for everyone presenting with a gender dysphoria, and this is the reason for the careful assessment process carried out by gender identity clinics. As already mentioned, about a quarter of the gender dysphoria patients I assessed for the psychotherapy service during the first ten-year period had previously undergone sex reassignment surgery, and did not find that it addressed their original experienced problem as anticipated. Many reported a sense of in-authenticity with regard to their post-operative gender identity, and once again reported *'not feeling right'* with the body they now had (we can consider this to be a 'transgender dysphoria').

Some give a history of unrealistic hopes of becoming the opposite sex, but never being accepted by others as an *'authentic'* woman (or man) after surgery. The challenge to their authenticity in their new gender may not be external. Many successfully *'pass'* in society: they look, and on the surface, behave like the man or woman they have chosen to be. However, they may *'read'* themselves as not legitimately belonging to that gender. In such instances, they report that the challenge comes from within them, as they have come to question the certainty they once had regarding their transgender identity.

PARALLEL PROCESSES

'Confusion', *'Binary Rigidity'*, *'Genital Centrality'*, and *'Questioning of Authenticity'*, as described above appear to be themes of psychological work with gender dysphoria. The examples outlined above hopefully indicate how these themes are observed to be occurring almost in parallel, not only with the person with gender dysphoria, but also relevant to the professionals and institutions professionally involved in their clinical care. It is in view of the 'parallel' nature of these observations that I coined the phrase 'parallel process' as a psychological term used to describe these themes occurring seemingly in parallel.

A PATIENT'S DREAM

The members of the therapy groups are encouraged to discuss issues from their everyday lives and also those arising from the interpersonal interactions, which occur in the process of the group sessions. Whilst the focus is very much on the 'here and now', occasionally a patient in the group will raise a dream they have had, and ask the other members and therapist for their thoughts in relation to it.

Working with 'the unconscious' is not a feature of the specially adapted therapeutic intervention and interpreting dreams is not a focus of the work as it is in other forms of analytic psychotherapy. However, the content of a dream may offer a relevant and useful vehicle for collaborative enquiry and consideration by the group members who can be invited to consider their own thoughts in connection with the dream being recollected.

In the following vignette, we return once again to Rose, who was originally referred for therapy due to her regrets of having had gender reassignment surgery and subsequent psychological ill-health. On this occasion, Rose arrived at a therapy session wanting to talk about a dream she'd had the night before.

> **Vignette:** In the dream there was a farmer, his 11-year-old son, and a sheep with wooden legs and calliper-like supportive devices on them. The farmer had put out hay for his sheep to eat (sheep do not eat hay, but this is a dream, and so of course, the usual rules do not apply). The farmer had put the hay for the sheep on top of a tall chimney. The sheep was struggling to climb up the chimney. In the dream, Rose tells the farmer that he has to kill the sheep, which the farmer does with a wooden mallet.

The group members discussed their thoughts about the dream Rose had described. Rose herself said that she had identified with the sheep, as she too had been 'modified' in some way. Another member suggested that Rose, like the farmer, had previously 'tried to kill off' an aspect of her identity and was once again trying to 'rid herself of what she had created of herself' as manifested by her thoughts about reverting to her male gender role. This member also stated that they could identify themselves with the wish to 'kill off' or 'rid' themselves of an identity. In the dream, the farmer's son was aged 11, which was coincidentally the same number of years ago when Rose had her gender reassignment surgery. The dream contained the common theme of the wish to rid oneself of unwanted aspects of oneself, which can be projected onto their bodies, which are then perceived as being in need of altering. In this instance, none of the suggested ideas came from the therapist; all the above-mentioned ideas (therapeutic interpretations) came from the group members themselves.

SPECIALIST PSYCHOTHERAPY FOR GENDER DYSPHORIA – A SUMMARY

Who is suitable for specially adapted group psychotherapy? People with gender identities that are less sustained, or do not fit into a binary male / female gender framework, those who do not wish to pursue physical treatments, and for whom sex reassignment has been unsuccessful in addressing their gender dissatisfaction or unhappiness, may all benefit, as described in this section. The main points of this section are listed in Table 7 below:

Table 7: Summary.

Not all people with gender dysphoria fit into a typical transgender presentation of a fixed gender identity corresponding to the opposite sex.
Hormones + surgical sex reassignment are useful for some but not all gender identity conditions.
For individuals with atypical gender identity presentations, a specially adapted group psychotherapy focussing on gender identity may be useful.
Features specific to the adapted model of psychotherapy include a collaborative and critical analytic enquiry into perceived gender constructs.
Particular features observed as specific to this work include the themes of binary rigidity, confusion, genital centrality, and questioning of authenticity of gender roles.
Professionals need to be wary of being drawn into polarised stances in relation to transgender politics and instead retain therapeutic neutrality and an open mind.

Psychotherapy and physical treatments are not mutually exclusive and many people with gender dysphoria wish to pursue both options concurrently. The psychotherapy as described in this section has clearly defined, explicit aims that are discussed and agreed with the person at the outset, and worked towards collaboratively throughout the treatment. Whilst many people presume that psychotherapy is an essential component of treatment for people referred for gender reassignment, this is unfortunately not the case. Psychotherapy is not routinely offered and where there is counselling available, it is generally of a supportive nature, helping people to acclimatise to a new gender role rather than aiming to help them acquire a greater sense of satisfaction and stability in their chosen gender, irrespective of whether this correlates with their biological sex. Through a careful exploration in group therapy of the meanings that members have afforded to gender in themselves and others, people are encouraged to evolve an individually tailored gender identity experienced as authentic to them. Patients are guided against attempts to assimilate into a perceived rigid binary gender framework in place of an identity specifically tailored to them, which may or may not fit within perceived conventional gender frameworks.

Psychotherapists working with gender dysphoria need to adopt an open and accepting attitude, as a formulaic approach can interfere with their understanding of a person's difficulties. Both therapists and patient need to differentiate between the concepts of 'sex' and 'gender,' the former having an organic basis and the latter being a psychosocial construct. Therapists must be open and accepting of transgender persons, who may not conform to a binary heterosexist framework of gender identity, and whose identities may be more fluid and indeterminate.

Clinicians should expect to encounter certain recurrent themes specific to working with gender dysphoria. These include binary rigidity, not only in relation to the person's relationship to gender, but also in how professionals may be drawn into (or perceived to be drawn into) polarised positions in relation to gender-reassignment surgery and transgender politics. Genital centrality may be manifest both in the person's relationship with their body, and also in the manner by which professionals may categorise patients and their suitability for therapy. People with gender dysphoria referred for psychotherapy often report concerns relating to the authenticity of their gender role. Sometimes, these concerns have remained after surgical sex reassignment. Unfortunately, services often deny transgender people the opportunity for psychotherapy, a rejection that is similar to the rejection a transgender person may have experienced in the past, in relation to aspects of themselves, their bodies or gender.

CHAPTER 10

CHILDREN WITH GENDER DYSPHORIA

The mere labelling of traits as masculine or feminine does not give either sex exclusive rights to them or even justify the broad division of traits between the sexes as a group.

Scheinfeld, 1944

Elizabeth Riley: It would be an understatement to say that parenthood represents a profound transition in a person's life. However, even more intense is the experience of parents whose children present with behaviour that is not only completely unexpected, but which is also, for most people, difficult to comprehend. This is the case for parents whose gender-variant children present with gender non-conformity on a spectrum ranging from cross-gender behaviour to a cross-sex identity. Cross-gendered behaviour challenges assumptions that an individual's gender presentation, behaviour, and preferences for particular activities are predicted by their physical sex. A cross-sex identity is indicated where the internal 'felt sex' identity is not congruent with the physical sex characteristics. *Gender dysphoria* is diagnosed where this incongruence between the body and true gender and sex identity causes significant distress.

Society is structured around a gender dichotomy of female / feminine and male / masculine identity and behaviour. This delineation of attributes and expectations about appearance and preferences imposes a great deal of pressure on gender variant children to conform. Not only do the consequences of this felt pressure negatively affect feelings of self-worth, they also cause significant suffering into adulthood. Furthermore, children with non-conforming gender identities or gender expression may experience marginalisation, rejection, abuse from family and peers, and may be subject to higher rates of depression, anxiety, and suicide. However, people with gender differences have existed around the world, throughout history, and variations in gender identity are proving to be a biological variation of human existence.

Over and above the pressures that all parents deal with, parents with gender variant children face the additional challenge of having to raise their child in a social service vacuum due to the lack of support available to them and their child. Although many parents raising gender variant children provide unconditional acceptance, love, and support, they may also be upset, confused, and overwhelmed by the recognition that their child is differently gendered, and may feel blamed or isolated due to the social stigma and secrecy surrounding gender-variance. Family or others' disapproval may trigger self-doubt in parenting skills and foster a shame response, particularly if they feel embarrassed by their child's gender expression. This may be further exacerbated by pressure to make decisions in their child's best interests before having had a chance to research and reflect on the situation, especially when their child believes they need their body to match their gender and sex identity. This chapter explores some common issues that arise when counselling parents raising gender variant children.

STARTING OUT

Parents' responses to a child's non-conforming gender behaviour or expression varies from unconditional support to denial, disbelief, shock, or punishment and many traverse a wide spectrum of reactions on the pathway to acceptance of their child. This pathway to acceptance has no formula and in many ways, it is developmental. Each family's needs and process will be a function of their culture, expectations, values, and beliefs, in conjunction with prior exposure to gender variance or associated concepts. The vignette below provides an example of a family attending counselling wanting support for their adolescent, who has recently disclosed a non-binary gender identification.

Parmen and Leona attended counselling with their adolescent daughter Martine, age 15.

PART 1: BACKGROUND

Martine (the youngest child with two older brothers) had been having trouble focusing at school and handing in assigned work. After seeing the school counsellor, when Martine had spoken about cutting, the counsellor contacted Martine's parents. Leona and Parmen were saddened to hear about Martine's distress and asked her what was wrong. Martine eventually replied that she thought they would not understand if her gender identity did not match their expectations of her as 'she' and as their 'daughter'. Martine explained the desire to change their name to be neutral, and that they wished to be referred to by third person pronouns: they, them, and their. Leona and Parmen were initially supportive in the hope that Martine would stop cutting and that the feelings would pass.

Martine continued to see the counsellor, but after a few months, her parents had reverted to using 'she'. Martine began having anxiety attacks and became withdrawn after a request to wear the neutral 'sport uniform' instead of the girl's uniform had been denied by her parents. The counsellor recommended that Leona and Parmen take Martine to a gender specialist for a gender identity assessment.

The gender specialist asked Leona, Parmen, and Martine what they wanted from the two-hour session. Leona replied that she couldn't make sense of Martine's request to be referred to as non-binary, that it 'didn't make sense' and that she wanted her daughter back. Parmen explained that he wanted to do what was best for Martine, that he was very concerned by the increasing withdrawal, and that he needed information to help him understand a 'different' gender identity. Martine said she was confused and wanted more information.

The clinician explained that first, they would speak to Leona and Parmen to understand their concerns and to get their perspective on Martine's history. Following this, they would speak to Martine to begin the gender identity assessment, and then for the last 15-minutes, they would bring Leona and Parmen in to discuss Martine's immediate needs, and assess what the next suitable steps could be.

When parents seek professional guidance, they may require education, validation, support, medical intervention, contact with other parents, referrals, guidance on parenting or some kind of intervention to help their child manage a social or medical transition. Parents who find their child's behaviour or identity distressing or unacceptable may also seek confirmation that their child is not gender variant, or does not have gender dysphoria. A social transition allows a child to live in their identified gender, acknowledging that some environments will be more accepting than others. Counselling helps the parents and child anticipate, prepare for, and negotiate challenges that may arise. Medical transition is indicated when the child is clearly identifying in the gender differing from the sex at birth, is socially transitioned (or wanting to transition) and is distressed by impending or actual changes in puberty. Medical transition requires specialists experienced in assessment of gender dysphoria and the administration of puberty blockers and hormones. This may include a supportive general practitioner, a counsellor / psychologist, a paediatric psychiatrist, and a paediatric endocrinologist.

In the process of accepting a child's variance from socially-constructed gender norms, parents may go through some periods of grief as well as a process of 'coming out' and integration. Initially, parents may reason that their child's beliefs or feelings about their identity or need for expression is a 'phase'. Alternatively, they may react with shock or express disbelief, especially as they struggle to reconcile what they 'know' about their child with what they are being told. What is often indicated by parents' responses is how deep their connection is to the birth-designated sex and gender of their child. In particular, if parents are unaware that a person's gender is individual and subjective, they may feel unable to let go of the expectations they hold about their child's future, and cope by simply ignoring it. In the past, they may have tried to steer their child into gender stereotypical activities or blamed the child for attention-seeking, stubbornness, or causing family disruption.

PART 2: INTERVIEW WITH PARENTS

Leona and Parmen described how Martine had been a happy child who had never caused them any trouble. They agreed that although she had never been a 'girly girl', she had close girlfriends. They recalled that, as a young child, Martine loved a 'tiger' outfit that she never wanted to take off, and would even wear it to bed. Leona explained: 'In primary school, she used to love soccer and we thought of her as a bit of a tomboy. When puberty came, she wore very girly clothes and stopped playing soccer. About a year later, she became very moody and would stay in her room for days when she had her period. Since then she has been a very picky eater and lost a lot of weight. I'm also worried that she is becoming anorexic as she now wears very baggy clothes and hunches to hide how skinny she is. I think she just doesn't want to grow up and got this idea off the internet.'

Recognising that their previous understandings of gender maintained a binary view that no longer fits with the reality of their child's gender and / or sex identity can be hard to deal with. Parents may begin to mourn the loss of the future expectations they had for their child. Additionally, they may feel a very personal 'loss' of the child they thought they knew. Parents may even encounter a 'loss of self,' losing confidence in their skills as parents as they begin to question their knowledge and beliefs.

In association with these losses, parents may also feel a sense of disorientation, instability, and ambiguity about an aspect of themselves and others that they had believed to be 'fixed'. Parents may also feel isolated from their regular networks, particularly if they don't know anyone with a similar experience. Access to other parents can provide immense comfort and validation as they expand their network of support.

Some parents voice concerns that their parenting inadvertently created their child's gender differences. Consequently, they may be anticipating and fearful of negative reactions and rejection from family, friends or local community. Therefore, it is important to let parents know about the naturally occurring nature of gender differences and the latest prevalence statistics. Some of their fears may be real; current research clearly shows elevated risks of harassment, bullying, attacks, and discrimination for children and young people with gender diversity (Hyde et al., 2014; Smith & Payne, 2015). One survey cited a parent's concern: 'We have been told how life will be hell for him and also for us if we continue to support him' (Riley et al., 2011).

Conversely, reactions of overprotectiveness and / or controlling the child to maintain secrecy about their gender variance may cause the child to feel ashamed. This kind of micro-parenting also appears to keep children young and dependant, preventing them from developing resilience.

PART 3: INTERVIEW WITH MARTINE

Martine described how, even though they were bullied by some girls for not liking the same things as a young child, they were happy-go-lucky, and could do whatever they wanted if they kept their hair long and wore dresses occasionally, to keep their parents happy. Martine explained that although they knew about puberty they just never really expected that it would happen to them, and they were 'horrified' when breasts began to develop. They described puberty as a 'nightmare that wouldn't go away, like something was happening to me ... like a punishment' and 'I kept trying to brush it off'. Martine said that they thought they had better 'try' to be a girl as that is what their body was, and they couldn't do anything about it. Martine said, 'pretending to be a girl didn't help at all, and only made me feel worse... Whenever I looked in the mirror I would see my body out of control and feel anxiety rising.' Martine spoke about how 'I don't eat or drink anything before or at school, as I don't want to go to the restroom. It feels wrong to go to the girls and I'd get beaten up if I went to the boys ... also I don't want bigger breasts'. Martine also disclosed that they hung out with friends instead of going to the recent swimming carnival as they could not bear to wear the girl's swimsuit. Martine said they loved it when their friends called them 'he' and 'Martin' but also that 'I don't think my parents would be able to handle me being a guy, it would hurt them so much and I feel so guilty already'. When asked what Martine wanted to happen they said, 'I want a proper binder (to help flatten my chest) instead of wearing three crop tops. I want my hair cut short. I want to wear the boys uniform at school. That would make my life a lot easier but I don't think my parents will agree'. The clinician sought Martine's approval to share with their parents the aspects of gender dysphoria that Martine was displaying and discussed which items Martine was not ready to disclose.

FACILITATING ACCEPTANCE

When parents are finding it difficult to appreciate and support their child's sense of self regarding gender and identity, counselling can promote honest and open conversations allowing the child's authenticity to shine through. Counselling professionals who prioritise connecting to the client's experience (over the rigid application of a technique, or stringently follow a particular therapeutic modality) can have more meaningful associations with their clients. This kind of collaborative engagement provides validation for parents and helps them to acknowledge their own issues regarding gender for the benefit of their child. Furthermore, once parents feel that their concerns have been understood they are more inclined to be empathic towards their child's perspective.

Providing information, resources, and education for parents on the experiences and needs of gender-variant children can also assist parents in understanding that their child's experiences and expressions are genuine. Recognising the similarities between their child and others may also help to encourage parents towards acceptance. Additionally, when a child's internal feelings are understood and reflected by their parents, their core sense of self and mental stability gets positive affirmation, helping them to develop their own sense of self-esteem.

Conversely, if parents are unable to reflect their child's reality, the child's self-confidence and self-trust is likely to suffer. For gender variant children, this is especially significant. They not only have to contend with developing a confident sense of self against the odds, they have also been taught by society not to trust feelings about their gender.

Once parents are able to establish that their child's beliefs are genuine, facilitating acceptance of their child's gender identity and / or expression becomes viable. Enquiring into the child's history, with a focus on gender and any associated feelings, whilst determining the intensity of the child's distress is a useful way to approach the assessment. These explorations provide the counsellor with key information that, with the child's permission, can be shared with parents to help them understand their child's needs. Showing respect for the parents' beliefs, expectations, and fears, as they strengthen their sensitivity to the child's feelings, helps to provide a stronger basis for the acceptance of the child.

PART 4: DISCUSSION WITH PARENTS AND MARTINE

The clinician explained to Leona and Parmen what gender dysphoria was, and what aspects of Martine's history indicated the existence of gender dysphoria and demonstrated needs for gender expression. The clinician discussed each aspect of Martine's expressed needs: to wear a binder, have their hair cut, and to wear the boys' school uniform. The clinician also showed Leona and Parmen some useful books for parents of teens, with variations in gender identity and expression, offered online and parent support networks, and suggested meeting again in a few weeks to follow up and check in with them and Martine.

Family discord regarding a child's gender can also provide challenges for parents. Not only can parents not prevent their child from experiencing hostility in the wider community, but their best care and support may not be enough to protect their child from other family members' reactions. Conflict can arise when parents recognise the difficulties of placating family members while advocating for their child. These conflicts may ultimately lead to estrangement from some family members. For example, one parent reported 'We choose to no longer spend time with the family as they think it is okay to say cruel things to us and our children' (Riley, et al. 2011). Consequently, parents may develop a fear of rejection and become secretive, mirroring their child's experience, which in itself reduces social support at a time when it is most needed.

Counselling can also help parents to regain their legitimate parental authority. At times, parents' compassion for their child's gender issues may result in them relaxing boundaries on: bedtimes, eating habits, computer use or school attendance, and / or allow the child's individual needs to take priority within the family (Pearlman, 2006). Once parental acceptance of the child's gender needs has been established, counselling can then help with the development of strategies for renewing mutual respect, allowing for reassertion of their parenting authority. Some of these strategies could include exploring past parent practices, or inviting comparisons of boundaries with other siblings, and encouraging discussions around how and why they feel their parenting ought to (or not) account for the child's gender needs. These interventions can allow parents to adjust their current parenting practices to make them more in line with their parenting beliefs and values.

Some parents, particularly those with older children experiencing gender dysphoria may want time to understand their child's condition and causation factors. However, having finally found a solution to their gender issues, the youth may be motivated to implement change as quickly as possible with little concern for potential outcomes. Parents on the other hand may be feeling extremely cautious, imploring their child to take time to properly consider their actions. They may feel that supporting their child's needs regarding gender is forcing them, as parents, to take action before they are ready. Rather, they would prefer their child to explore other avenues, for fear their child is making a mistake. Addressing the parents' concerns (as above) while ensuring that multiple professionals are assessing the child may help them to recognise appropriate ways to support their child's immediate needs.

Parents may also request support to help their child's social transition at school. This may include referrals to services that provide training, education and information to school staff and parents. A school providing training in this way helps the child to have a positive attitude towards school while supporting them both socially and academically. Also, schools that employ anti-bullying and harassment programmes find that their students are more likely to feel a sense of belonging. A comprehensive training program ensures that the child's social transition is facilitated in a trans-positive, gender diverse, and safe environment while securing the best protection and support for both the child and their family.

SUMMARY – CHILDREN WITH GENDER DYSPHORIA

Parents raising children with differences in gender identity or gender expression most often find themselves managing a situation that is not only outside of their experience but also beyond their imagination.

Counselling professionals have a responsibility to help parents understand their own needs as well as their child's, while also helping them manage their role as parents. Welcoming their perspectives and allowing them to express their fears and concerns fosters a climate of acceptance and empowerment, helping parents set realistic goals and respond in their child's best interests. Valuing parents' skills and strengths can provide a useful contrast against judgements made by others, and encourage parents' awareness, understanding and acceptance of themselves. Meanwhile, respecting expressions of loss and grief can also help parents to gain confidence and help them to construct or maintain healthy family dynamics and reduce instability in the family system. Parents are also likely to appreciate any support that counsellors can offer in finding networks of other parents raising children with differences in gender identity or expression.

Externally, parents may find themselves advocating for their child in schools and local communities in order to create safe environments, while protecting their child from negativity. Counsellors can help here by providing up-to-date information, resources, and referrals to other gender identity professionals.

In summary, providing the necessary information and referrals while facilitating parental confidence, support networks, and acceptance of their child's needs, offers parents a solid foundation for their future journey in supporting and advocating for their child.

SECTION 3
CHANGING SEX

CHAPTER 11

GENDER IDENTITY CLINIC SERVICES IN THE UK

 Most people with gender dysphoria, who are looking to pursue physical interventions in order to reassign their gender, will go to a gender identity clinic, which will link up to other specialist services.

In this chapter and the next, we'll look at services offered in the UK and Australia, and I am grateful to Kevan Wylie and Fintan Harte for their overview of gender identity services on opposite sides of the world.

 Professor Kevan Wylie: Most people with gender dysphoria, who are looking to pursue physical interventions in order to reassign their gender, will go to a gender identity clinic, which will link up to other specialist services.

In this chapter and the next, we'll look at services offered in the UK and Australia, and I am grateful to Kevan Wylie and Fintan Harte for their overview of gender identity services on opposite sides of the world.

INTRODUCTION

In this chapter, we'll present an overview of the various clinical services that are provided within the United Kingdom, for patients with gender dysphoria and related clinical symptoms. I'll outline how patients are referred to specialist services, the assessment process, and the treatment options that are available in clinics. I will also outline the various treatments that are available for the transition of gender, including psychological therapies, hormonal therapies, and surgical treatments.

In 2013, there were two important changes to the provision of services for gender dysphoria in the United Kingdom. The first of these was the release of the Good Practice Guidelines (CR181) document, produced by a committee involving representatives from several medical royal colleges, clinical societies and associations, and service users, including advocacy groups. These standards provide guidance to clinicians about best contemporary practice and the management of patients with gender dysphoria, and the guidance is referenced throughout this chapter. Although there are many areas of commonality, the guidelines are distinct from the international guidelines issued by the World Professional Association for Transgender Health (WPATH). The UK Guidelines are followed by clinicians working in the United Kingdom, as these have the endorsement of a number of its medical royal colleges.

The second major change is the commissioning, in England, of gender dysphoria services in accordance with criteria outlined in a document by the National Health Service (NHS) commissioning board. The NHS commissioning board is committed to ensuring equality of access and non-discrimination, irrespective of age, disability, gender reassignment, marriage and civil partnership, pregnancy and maternity, race, religion or belief, sex (gender) or sexual orientation.

PRELIMINARY ASSESSMENT

Regardless of location, access to a gender identity service should be within reasonable travelling distance and time. The number of services across the United Kingdom is limited, with specialist identity clinics currently based in Exeter, Leeds, London, Newcastle, Northampton, Nottingham, and Sheffield in England. In addition, services exist in Aberdeen, Edinburgh, Glasgow, and Inverness for Scotland, and in Belfast for Northern Ireland. Limited services are also available in Wrexham for residents of Wales. Waiting times for access are similar to those for other patients attending tertiary clinics. Specialist gender clinics provide patients and referrers with details about their services and protocols. Individuals attending gender identity services should be referred by their doctor, or via a psychologist, non-specialist psychiatrist, or sexual health centre via a GP to the gender service provider. It is usual practice that the doctor will enter into collaborative care arrangements with the gender service.

The purpose of the preliminary assessment is to identify if any mental health diagnoses exist, and to obtain an opinion about how the patients' needs may best be met from a range of options. Regardless of the service of referral, treatment in the field is holistic insofar as different specialties are usually involved. It is not necessary that all of these specialists work together within the same building, but the establishment of local protocols for interdisciplinary and multi-disciplinary working should be clear for service users. Choices of treatments and the sequencing of treatment with individual service providers allows for a flexible approach to care. In particular, the concept that many individuals may not find themselves conforming to the binary male or female role should be accepted, recognising that for some, neutralising treatments are the preferred way forward.

Most services require a period of assessment, during which psychological assessment will take place. This will include a general medical and mental health assessment, and more specifically, a review of lifelong function, including any history of psychological or medical conditions. Childhood behaviours, adolescent cross-dressing, and adult relationships will be recorded. Some patients may already have transitioned in gender role and this will be an area of specific enquiry. Administration of hormones is no longer dependent on the person having already lived in the new gender role, and increasingly, services are getting more flexible in offering hormonal therapy once the assessment period is complete, even if the gender role change has not yet taken place. When this gender role change has not taken place, a clearly documented treatment plan and regular reviews should be scheduled in the medical record. Attention should be given to family, relationship, social and vocational matters.

For people under the age of 17 years, patients are referred to specialist services; there is one remaining national unit at the Tavistock and Portman NHS Trust, and a regional service at Leeds. Between the ages of 17 years, and 17 years 6 months, discussion with the young person and their carers should take place before stating a preferred service for referral. People over 17 years and 6 months are referred into a relevant adult service.

LIVING IN THE GENDER CONGRUENT ROLE

This may be challenging for some individuals and can have profound personal and social consequences as well as an impact on vocation. The awareness of the impact on the family, relationships, education, vocation, as well as economic and legal challenges are all important considerations that the individual may be supported with during the period of transition. The duration of 12 months is considered to be sufficient time for different life experiences and events throughout the year including university or work experiences, holidays, and family events. Patients should present consistently across all settings in life in their desired gender role. Specific advice from NHS Scotland makes note that patients will be required to provide the gender clinic with verification that they are living and working in a particular gender role. This proof can be given by means of collateral interviews, official documentation from employers and educational institutions, or from other formal organisations. The gender identity clinic may consider the experience should be extended if they or the patient feel that further time is needed, or if attendance at the service has been inconsistent.

Many individuals will arrange for a change of name by Deed Poll or statutory declaration. Copies of this should be kept within the patient record. For many people, the gender role change occurs at around the same time as the prescription of hormones. However, some services will require individuals to live full-time in the preferred gender role, before agreeing to prescribe hormones, whilst other services will adopt a more flexible approach. It's important there should be a record in the case file showing that the patient has experienced persistent gender dysphoria prior to the prescription of any endocrine treatment. This gender dysphoria can be identified and confirmed in a number of ways. These may include sessions with a psychiatrist with specialist experience in diagnosing and managing gender dysphoria, or from a clinical psychologist with similar experience. For others, a period of time in psychotherapy with either a psychotherapist or a counsellor may be necessary for the confirmation of gender dysphoria to be established. Thereafter, a diagnosis of gender dysphoria (DSM-5) or transsexualism (ICD-10) will usually be established although increasingly, variations to these diagnoses are accepted as legitimate for treatment to be offered.

ENDOCRINE TREATMENTS

Provision of (hormone) treatments is usually made following a single opinion from a member of a gender identity team or network.

Hormone prescribing usually takes place under the guidance of specialist services, mainly in primary care. For some individuals, the changes brought about by endocrine treatment may be sufficient that they choose not to undergo further social change, or any surgery. Hormone support is undertaken as part of a clinical process involving a clinical endocrinologist or specialist in sexual or reproductive medicine who has obtained informed consent. Alternatively, using clearly developed protocols, as advised within Standards of Care documents, a doctor may prescribe medication with access to an endocrinologist or sexual medicine specialist as necessary. Full discussion of fertility issues should precede all endocrine treatments, giving opportunities for egg / sperm storage for possible use in the future, although this is not usually funded within the UK. Physical assessment and ongoing haematological, endocrine and biochemical monitoring is essential, using agreed collaborative care protocols. Regular reviews are essential. The choice of actual hormone preparation alongside the method of delivery and dosage should be in line with current understanding of minimum health risks and maximum efficacy.

Clinicians should discourage patients from using hormones obtained from the internet or other sources. For trans women, the mainstay of therapy is oestrogen therapy, with suppression of androgen secretion and action. For trans men, the mainstay of therapy is androgen therapy, with suppression of oestrogen secretion and action. The use of a gonadotropin-releasing hormone agonist suppresses sex steroid secretion and action. Some clinics offer agents that have an anti-androgen effect, including cyproterone and spironolactone. The use of certain medications is sometimes indicated when there is scalp hair loss, although there are increasing concerns about the long term effects on both sexuality and cognition following use of these agents. Regular monitoring is advisable and may, for example, identify a raised haematocrit in trans men (from androgen therapy) but this is usually manageable with venesection under the care of a haematologist.

SURGICAL INTERVENTIONS

Eligibility criteria for gender reassignment surgery requires:

- A competence to consent to receive treatment consistent with safe clinical practice and relevant legislation.
- 12 months of continuous endocrine therapy (for those without medical contraindication).
- A similar period of at least 12 months continuous living in the gender congruent role.
- Demonstrable knowledge of the length of period of hospitalisation alongside possible complications limitations and post-surgical requirements.

Patients with the gender recognition certificate should have this taken into account during the referral process. In addition, readiness criteria include demonstrable progress in consolidating one's gender identity role; and demonstrable progress in dealing with external social, family and interpersonal issues resulting in an improved state of mental health.

For some trans men whose breasts are causing them distress, they may have chest reconstruction around the same time as the change in gender role. For some patients, breast binders may be sufficient in the short term, but for others, binders may restrict the breathing process and damage breast tissue. This may complicate the results of chest surgery. Administration of testosterone for six-months before any chest surgery usually improves the outcome of the surgery.

Genital reconstructive surgery is offered in the main centres of London, Brighton, Leicester, and Leeds. Chest surgery may be offered by specialist surgeons more local to the trans person's home. Hysterectomy and removal of the whole reproductive system may also be provided if indicated.

Arrangements for cessation of hormones prior to arrival at hospital, and for planned aftercare, first with a district nurse and then by members of the gender team should be part of a well-planned package of care.

ADDITIONAL SERVICES

A number of factors are conducive to a successful outcome although these are not all necessarily available at each gender service. Peer support is valuable, using both self-help service resources and groups, as well as those that may be offered within gender identity clinics. Support for families is also helpful. The Gender Identity Research and Education Society (GIRES) offers support to families, as well as providing wider information about trans issues. Facial and body hair removal, and provision of hair-pieces, is often important, particularly for trans women. One essential aspect of treatment for many male-to-female (MtF) patients is removal of facial hair which impacts on confidence during the preoperative 12 months' experience. Electrolysis, laser, and Intense Pulse Light (IPL) treatments may be funded for a limited number of sessions (sessions will only be unlimited in the case of donor skin that will be used for gender confirmatory surgery). The related benefits of providing support on image in the new gender social role are seen as particularly useful for patients who may make use of an image consultant. Voice and communication skills are an important part of the transition; input from speech and language therapists is particularly useful. For those who are finding difficulties with employment, and the transition into the gender congruent role, services from psychotherapists and occupational therapists during the transition period can be valuable. Other surgeries such as tracheal shave, cricothyroid reduction, and facial feminisation may be sought by some patients but these are not usually funded by the NHS.

THE GENDER RECOGNITION ACT 2004

This Act provides full legal recognition for transgender people who have acquired a gender status. This means that people who have taken decisive steps to change their gender role permanently are afforded all of the same rights and responsibilities as other individuals in that gender. The Act allows trans people to establish "for all purposes" their identified gender status by obtaining a gender recognition certificate. This allows trans people to marry according to their acquired gender status. If the individual was born within the UK, a new birth certificate is issued. The gender recognition panel requires evidence that the individual has had, or has gender dysphoria, and has lived in the new gender role for two years prior to making the application – and intends to live permanently in the new gender role. There is also the stipulation that the person should be at least 18 years old and not in a pre-existing marriage or civil partnership. If such a relationship does occur this must be annulled before the full GRC is awarded. It is not a requirement that genital surgery has taken place.

THE EQUALITY ACT 2010

Discrimination, victimisation, and harassment because of gender reassignment are prohibited under this Act, both in employment and in the provision of goods, facilities, services, and access to facilities. The protected characteristic of gender reassignment applies if the person is proposing to undergo, is currently undergoing, or has already undergone a process for the purpose of reassigning their sex by changing physiological or other attributes of sex. The protection applies from the point of disclosing this intention.

CHAPTER 12

GENDER IDENTITY SERVICES IN AUSTRALIA

 **Dr Fintan Harte:** In this chapter, I will outline a broad range of transgender services both professional and community-based in Australia. National and state services will also be listed at the end of the chapter.

BACKGROUND

Transgender services in Australia date back to the 1960s. At that time, only limited psychological and endocrinological (hormone) services, and very limited gender reassignment surgery services were being provided by a small number of medical practitioners working in isolation. Similarly, those limited services were only available to a small number of people with intense gender dysphoria – to reiterate, that refers to people experiencing intense distress between their experienced gender and the gender they were assigned at birth. In the 1960s, those people would have been diagnosed as being 'true transsexuals' and only those experiencing intense gender dysphoria would have been offered sex reassignment surgery 'as a treatment of last resort'. Very often this would have been carried out in secret, for fear of disapproval from the more conservative medical and psychiatric establishment of the day.

Over the last 50 years, we have seen a diverse range of services develop in all states and territories in Australia, catering to an even more diverse range of gender variant identified and gender questioning individuals. Legal recognition of the rights of trans-identified individuals and an increasing awareness of the availability of both community and professional support has helped. It has led to a marked increase in the number of people requesting access to transgender services and pursuing psychological and physical treatments, in keeping with their experienced and self-affirmed gender identities.

ONLINE SERVICES

For many people questioning their gender identity, online support services may be their primary source of information. While many websites provide accurate information on gender diversity, they may not be the most appropriate source of information for a young person who is questioning their gender identity. Finding an experienced trans-friendly family doctor / general practitioner online is a good starting point. These professionals should be able to start the process of helping a person explore their gender identity. Alternatively, the health practitioner may prefer to refer the client to an experienced counsellor / psychologist / psychiatrist who has experience in transgender issues. Similarly, community mental health centres and local sexual health centres may be able to guide a person in the direction of appropriate gender specialists if they do not have the appropriate expertise.

Community-based organisations can be a tremendous source of support and information. They may be able to direct people to professional services that meet their needs, and provide peer support which is often beneficial for individuals who are gender questioning and may want to consider gender transition.

THE GENDER SPECIALIST

The aforementioned services may refer a client for assessment by a gender specialist: a health professional who has spent many years assessing people with gender variance, and who has a caseload of gender variant individuals constituting a significant proportion of their clinical practice. Consequently, they are deemed to have expertise in the assessment of people with gender confusion, people who may be gender questioning and those with affirmed alternative gender identities.

Gender specialists can come from a variety of disciplines including general practice / family medicine, counselling psychologists, clinical psychologists, social workers, mental health nurses, and psychiatrists. All of these specialists are qualified to explore gender diversity in a psychotherapeutic context, but only some write letters of recommendation for physical treatments including hormones and surgery.

THE GENDER ASSESSMENT

People may present to a mental health professional at various stages of gender exploration. Some present in the early stages, wanting to explore aspects of gender expression. Others present with requests for specific physical treatments for gender transition, e.g. hormones and surgery, having already explored their gender variance and affirmed their desire for physical treatments appropriate to their gender needs. This is the first step to be clarified in the therapeutic interaction with the gender specialist, i.e. the goals of the patient.

Assessment services in Australia adhere to the international standards of care of WPATH (World Professional Association for Transgender Health). The most recent standards of care, SOC 7, were published at the WPATH symposium held in Atlanta, USA, in September 2011 and are available at www.wpath.org.

The standards of care recognise the rights of people to affirm their chosen gender identity. The standards also recognise that, prior to accessing irreversible medical treatments for transgender, applicants should undergo a comprehensive psychosocial evaluation by an appropriately qualified mental health professional. This will establish the stability of a person's affirmed gender identity. People can present to mental health professionals with gender identity confusion, which can reflect a range of underlying alternative psychiatric and psychological conditions that do not reflect a core gender identity issue. While these conditions are not common, they are nonetheless, an important alternative diagnosis to gender dysphoria and need to be excluded prior to people undertaking irreversible transgender treatments. Clinical conditions encountered by gender specialists in these circumstances include long-standing psychosis, general identity problems, dissociative identity disorders, severe intellectual disability, and a number of other severe psychiatric problems. Any of these might preclude an individual's ability to give informed consent to irreversible gender reassignment treatments. In addition, mental health professionals assessing people with gender dysphoria may encounter other psychiatric conditions requiring treatment. It is important that such conditions are adequately treated and resolved prior to undertaking the potential stress of gender transition. Gender transition can prove stressful for many individuals, so it's important that they are supported throughout the process.

THE GENDER DYSPHORIA CLINIC

Victoria was the first state in Australia with a government-funded gender dysphoria clinic. The funding facilitates employment of staff including a secretary, social worker, clinical psychologist, speech pathologist, and psychiatrists. Referrals are made to endocrinologists and plastic surgeons in the private sector.

Other states and territories in Australia offer gender dysphoria assessment services and you can find their contact details on the Australian and New Zealand Professional Association for Transgender Health website – www.anzpath.org. However, we'll use the Victorian Gender Dysphoria Clinic as an example to demonstrate how many of these assessment services operate.

When a client applies to the Victorian Gender Dysphoria Clinic they will receive an information pack explaining the clinic's protocol. This will ask the client to obtain a referral from their usual doctor, or other medically qualified person. In addition, clients will be asked to write a brief autobiographical narrative (between 600 and 750 words is recommended) detailing the nature of their gender dysphoria and how it has affected their life. This gives the assessment team an overall view of how gender dysphoria has impacted on the client's life and their goals for treatment. It also gives the client the opportunity to explore the nature of their gender identity. Externalising these thoughts in written form can be therapeutic and may help the client clarify their goals for gender expression and / or gender transition. Patients who have a longstanding and strongly affirmed gender identity, and no complicated psychiatric history, may only require limited psychiatric assessment.

THE ASSESSMENT PROCEDURE

Mental health professionals will see clients for a number of assessment sessions. The number of sessions will vary depending on the complexity of the client's mental health history. Someone with a complex psychiatric history, including multiple psychiatric hospitalisations, suicide attempts, and treatment with a range of psychotropic medications will require more extensive psychiatric evaluation than somebody who has never needed to see a mental health professional, has never had a psychiatric hospitalisation, and has never been treated with psychotropic medications, or required extensive psychotherapy. Clients who present as psychologically stable, with no psychiatric history, and who are clear in their goals for gender transition, may end up having a time limited mental health evaluation.

The initial mental health assessment focuses on the nature of the gender dysphoria and how it has affected the person's life. This will include discussion on the intensity of the gender dysphoria, the development of gender dysphoria over the person's lifespan, and the reaction of family and partners to the manifestation of the disclosed or discovered gender variance. The person's ability to cope with adverse reactions to the expression of their preferred / affirmed gender identity is also explored. Gender dysphoria often increases in intensity with the onset of puberty which can have a significant negative impact on a person's overall mental health. It may prove beneficial to discuss this in therapy.

Another important issue is how the person wishes to express their gender variance. This may vary from presenting full-time in the affirmed gender role, to episodic presentation in an alternative gender to the assigned birth gender, in private or in public.

It is important to remember that over the period of gender assessment, it may become clear to both the gender specialist and the client that the underlying gender variance is symptomatic of something other than a core gender identity issue. In these cases, it is important for both the health professional and patient to explore the treatment options available in an ongoing psychotherapeutic relationship.

In Gender Dysphoria Clinics, which have clinical psychologists on staff, patients who have co-existing psychiatric problems (in addition to their gender dysphoria) may be referred for more in-depth psychological testing. Such testing is always carried out with a view to clarifying the clinical issues and to assist in treatment. It is never undertaken to preclude access to gender reassignment treatments.

HORMONE TREATMENT

Hormones are chemicals that occur naturally in the human body. They are responsible for many of the changes that take place at puberty. In natal females, oestrogens cause breast development and the onset of the menstrual cycle. In natal males, testosterone causes body hair growth, deepening of the voice pitch, and increased muscular strength. Hormone treatment for many clients is an essential step in the gender transitioning process. Prior to hormone initiation, patients need to undergo a psychosocial and medical evaluation to establish that there is no contraindication to undergoing hormonal gender reassignment from a psychological and a medical perspective. Hormones have potentially serious side-effects so it is essential that clients starting hormone treatment undergo medical evaluation. This will include a physical examination and baseline blood tests. Some clients feel this is an unnecessary procedure, but undergoing a psychosocial and medical evaluation prior to beginning hormone therapy is a good way of excluding a number of medical contraindications to hormone treatment, and potentially avert adverse events. Excessive oestrogen use can lead to thromboembolism, pulmonary embolism, and death. Similarly, excessive testosterone use can lead to liver damage. So prescription of hormones needs to be carefully monitored with regular blood tests, and self-initiation of prescribed substances from illicit sources online is strongly discouraged.

Many clients are satisfied with hormonal gender reassignment, and after appropriate psychosocial and medical evaluation, decide that they do not wish to proceed to surgical gender reassignment procedures. In Australia, access to hormonal treatment is in keeping with the WPATH international standards of care. A letter of recommendation from a suitably qualified mental health professional is required. The patient needs to be legally emancipated in the state of jurisdiction and capable of giving informed consent. If there are any medical or psychiatric conditions present, they need to be reasonably well controlled. In some Australian jurisdictions, patients with a complicated psychiatric history may be referred to a second mental health professional for a second opinion, prior to approval for hormone treatment. Negative prognostic features in patients undergoing oestrogen therapy include obesity, smoking, a history of blood-clots or a past history of cardiovascular disease.

SURGICAL TREATMENTS

A range of surgical treatments are available for gender variant individuals in Australia. For male to female patients, these can include a range of facial feminisation surgeries, including hair transplants, reduction of frontal bossing (the bony prominences above the eyebrows), cheek implants, rhinoplasty, thyroid cartilage reduction (Adam's apple), and a range of collagen and botox injections designed to achieve a more feminine facial appearance. Breast augmentation surgery may be an option for those patients who do not achieve satisfactory breast growth with hormone treatment alone after a recommended period of time. Finally, genital gender reassignment surgery may include a variety of techniques, the principal ones being (1) penile inversion technique and (2) colono-vaginoplasty.

For female to male patients, routine surgeries available in Australia include chest reconstruction surgery, hysterectomy, and bilateral salpingo oophorectomy (removal of fallopian tubes and ovaries). 'Bottom surgeries' including total vaginectomy, metoidioplasty (creation of a micropenis), testicular implants, and phalloplasty are less available. The success rate for many bottom surgeries is less than optimal. Consequently, many surgeons are reluctant to undertake these surgical procedures in Australia at this time. Similarly, patients are also reluctant to undertake these often expensive surgical procedures that have a limited guarantee of successful outcomes.

As for the requirements for hormone treatment, most Australian jurisdictions will follow the recommendations of the WPATH international standards of care to access surgical treatments. For chest reconstruction surgery, in female to male transsexuals, this requires one letter of referral from a suitably qualified mental health professional that has carried out a comprehensive psychosocial evaluation. For those patients requiring genital gender reassignment surgeries, two letters of referral from appropriately qualified mental health professionals are required. Where one referral is from a mental health professional with a Master's degree in a clinical behavioural science, the other referral must be from a mental health professional holding a doctoral qualification in either psychiatry or clinical psychology. Clients may elect to have a range of surgical procedures in order to enhance their physical appearance and improve their self-image. The degree to which clients pursue such surgical interventions is variable.

OUTCOMES

Outcome data for the various trans health treatments offered in Australia is lacking. Anecdotally, the regret rate for the various interventions on offer would appear to be low, in keeping with other internationally reported regret rates. Conversely, the satisfaction rate would appear to be quite high.

Research into patient satisfaction, carried out by the author and colleagues at a multidisciplinary gender dysphoria clinic in Melbourne, showed 80% of clients expressed overall satisfaction with the service. Clinician's knowledge and understanding was rated very highly, and clients reported a significant reduction in their gender related distress, as a result of attending the clinic. Research relating to satisfaction with specific transgender treatments and surgery is yet to be carried out in Australia.

CHAPTER 13

CROSS-SEX HORMONE THERAPY

 Rosemary Jones: Cross-sex hormone therapy is medication that is introduced to an individual with gender dysphoria that will change their appearances and functioning from the natal (birth) sex to the characteristics of the individual sex desired. Cross-sex hormone therapy can follow on the more modern concept of puberty blockade in a child, which may commence at the age of 18 in Australia, but earlier elsewhere. That age is the subject of continuing discussion and contention with the Family Law Courts in various countries. The aim for the future is to start the hormones at the time of puberty to enable natural development of the body and mind towards the desired sex.

Therapy for one or the other sex is totally different. Of course, different hormones are used, and the introduction of cross-sex hormone therapy for trans men is very much easier than it is for trans women.

The main objective for a trans man is to suppress the ovarian function so that there is no longer a menstrual cycle and, more importantly, no menstrual bleed which is anathema to a trans man.

The second aim would be to suppress further breast growth. That is likely to be more or less successful, depending on the age at which any hormonal therapy is given. In the mature individual, at about the age of perhaps 18 or 19, the breasts will have fully developed, and will require surgical attention to restore the chest to a male chest.

In terms of the strength of hormone production, the ovaries are quite weak compared to the power of testes producing testosterone. So, there is very little need to blockade the function of the ovaries thanks to the blocking effect of testosterone. In terms of the developmental effects of testosterone, the aim is that the individual puts on more muscle, the body will become more defined, with some reduction of body fat, which may be converted into muscle. It is to be expected that facial hair growth will be quite vigorous, allowing that trans man to grow a beard, and there may be an increase in body hair growth, perhaps on the chest, tummy, and the legs. It would be expected that the face and hair would become more oily; indeed the downside of testosterone is that the individual may develop acne of the face which can be severe. Low dose antibiotics, such as Minocycline can help clear it up. There will be a distinct stimulation of the clitoris and vulva, and the clitoris can enlarge to as much as 3-4cm which may give the impression of an undeveloped penis. If the stimulation is excessive then the clitoris can become sore, signalling the need to lower the dose of testosterone.

It is not desirable to administer testosterone by mouth as the data in the literature suggests that it would put the individual at an increased risk of primary hepatoma (cancer of the liver). The risk is very tiny but disappears altogether when testosterone is given by implant, or more commonly, by injection. These injections become known as 'the shots' and may be administered by a doctor, nurse, or indeed a close friend. They can also be administered by the patient himself, injecting into the front of the thigh. The frequency of injections varies from individual to individual but, in general, no one should receive more than one shot every two weeks, and in some cases, one every three weeks is preferred. After the shot, it is important not to allow a rundown in testosterone status towards the end of the duration, as that gives a subjective effect of downturn or disruption of mood reminiscent of the menstrual cycle. So it is best to give the shots in a 'top and tail' pattern of administration for sustained absorption. Once the desired effects are achieved, in terms of development, the dose of testosterone can be reduced to a maintenance dose. This is best achieved by continuing with long term Depot injections, or indeed transdermal testosterone in patch or gel form. The patches have a high rate of skin irritation and are not favoured. But some people also dislike the gel as it strikes them as being a bit 'feminine'. It can also take quite a while to dry and become effective. A spray product has now been introduced, which may be applied into the armpit daily. Testosterone implants vary in their availability and can be quite expensive.

There are few risks associated with testosterone treatment for trans men. All sex steroids, including testosterone, can affect liver function. So blood tests to check liver function should be carried out perhaps once a year. Testosterone has the capacity to increase the concentration of red blood cells, and if the count rises too high then the dose of testosterone should be reduced, or the individual trans man should take daily aspirin to prevent the theoretical risk of so-called 'sludging of the blood'. What this means is that the blood becomes thicker and more concentrated so that it moves less easily through the small blood vessels, leading to the theoretical possibility of blockage of the small blood vessels. This is mainly theoretical and I am not aware of any certain reports of this in clinical practice.

The regime for the trans woman is more complex with the difficulty arising from the fact that the testes are incredibly powerful organs. In the natal male, testes produce 12 times as much testosterone as in the natal female. These runaway trucks of organs require firm suppression with medication. This is done mainly by employing a substance in the so-called anti-androgen group of drugs (chemical castration). There are two main classes of this drug: Spironolactone (commonly referred to as Spiro), and Androcur (otherwise called Cyproterone). Spiro is generally prescribed as a blood pressure controlling medication and indeed one of the side-effects of Spiro is that the blood pressure can become too low, leaving the individual feeling a little faint from time to time. It does have the advantage of being accessible and cheap. Androcur is a very powerful anti-androgen which, for some reason is not officially favoured in some parts of the world but is a very powerful anti-testosterone medication. These substances can reduce the testosterone level and availability to zero. In addition, the 'reception' of testosterone onto its tissue receptor may be blocked. While that might seem an attractive idea to the emerging trans woman, it can leave that individual completely bereft of testosterone. In itself that can instigate symptoms similar to that of a psychological depression. Mainly it is that the mood becomes upset and energy levels completely dissipate. It is fundamental to the trans woman's transition that the testosterone level is reduced, so that hair growth on the face will be retarded, and erections will cease. Indeed, it is a reliable marker of the effectiveness of treatment when the individual no longer has erections when waking in the morning ('morning glories') and is unable to instigate an erection. The facial hair growth will continue, if slightly softened, but will require treatment by laser and electrolysis to get rid of it altogether.

Having thus dealt with one part of the pharmacological attack – the suppression of the natal gonads – the other half of the equation concerns the instigation and encouragement of feminine development. This is where oestrogen treatment plays its part.

The questions then are, what substance to choose, in what dosage and by what route? It has, in the past, been common practice to use the oestrogen that is found in the oral contraceptive (ethinyloestradiol). But the use of this hormone has come under such a cloud internationally that it has been universally discarded because of the demonstrated dangers. For example, it is no longer available as an oestrogen to be marketed to postmenopausal women as Hormone Replacement Therapy. Less dangerous are those oestrogens, which are generally termed 'natural oestrogens,' as opposed to the synthetic and very powerful nature of ethinyloestradiol. It should be noted however, that even the natural oestrogens are not without their risks. The major risk is an increased risk of blood clots. These can occur as a deep vein in the leg, known as a deep vein thrombosis (DVT), this results in the risk that a clot may break off and become lodged within the lungs, causing death. The second most common blood clot occurs within the brain and may cause a stroke. Blood clots however can occur elsewhere in the body, as happened to one of my patients. It should be clearly understood by all trans women that the use of oestrogens is attended by the risk of complications, including the rare risk of death. That was always the case with the oral contraceptive for young women, and that risk was justified on the grounds that the risk of death from pregnancy was higher than that from using the pill. The same argument cannot be applied to a trans woman, in terms of pregnancy risk at least. But it may equally apply in terms of the necessity for a trans woman to have oestrogen to achieve the body she requires to conform to her self-perception, and achieve peace of mind in how she presents. The flip side of this argument is that if the trans person remains untreated, she has a significantly increased risk of self-harm and suicide (42.5% risk – The First Australian National Trans Mental Health Study).

There are other risks of administered oestrogen such as gall bladder disease, tumours of the pituitary gland within the brain, and rarely arterial blood clots.

Generally speaking, the oestrogen of choice is oestradiol or 17 beta oestradiol, and that is given by mouth in doses that are about six times larger than one would give to a menopausal woman for hormone replacement. I usually start the trans woman on tablet oestrogen for a couple of months to let her familiarise herself with the feel of the hormone and then at the end of that period of time, start on the anti-androgen, usually Androcur. At the end of three months I would ordinarily put in an oestrogen implant, continue the anti-androgen and gradually reduce the oral oestrogen. To me, this administration protocol carries the least risk.

From time to time, there may be the need to instigate screening investigations, particularly if there appears to be a problem. General health screening should continue with a look at the lipids, the liver function tests, and the haemoglobin, particularly for the trans men, along with continuing assessment of bone density and blood tests to assess the extent of bone destruction. A well-informed doctor will do this quite automatically and easily.

The question of whether a trans man should continue to have cervical smear tests and the decision about whether or not to do this has been influenced, in recent years, by the introduction of HPV immunisation; the expectation is that there will be no further abnormal smears. If the adult individual has not had all three injections, he should be strongly encouraged to go and receive them. To undertake a vaginal examination in a trans man is often a critically difficult experience for the man, and best confined to the symptomatic patient. I do still offer vaginal examinations and smear tests, but in a way that leaves it very open for them to refuse without any upset.

With the introduction of surgery and the abolition of the gonads, the therapeutic situation becomes far easier, and puts the trans woman exactly and squarely in the class of a castrated cis woman (born woman) in the menopause. Once body morphology has been modified and transition can be considered complete, she can go on to standard support with hormones, as with any other woman suffering the castrate menopause. While in America there is a great enthusiasm for undertaking hysterectomies and removal of both ovaries, I find it difficult to endorse that for trans men. Of course, from time to time, an attempt should be made to exclude new pathology in those genitalia, but failing that, I can't see a good reason for elective surgery. An exception to that would be the occasional individual who is dead-set on having everything remotely resembling femininity removed from his newly masculine body.

CHAPTER 14

SURGICAL PROCEDURES

 WARNING: This chapter contains graphic images of genitalia.

GENDER SURGERY

 Andrew Ives: Gender surgery is a recognised treatment modality for patients suffering with gender dysphoria. It is often the last step for many patients in their journey.

The surgery can be divided in several ways; genital and non-genital procedures, and male-to female, and female to male procedures.

A) MALE TO FEMALE

1) GENITAL SURGERY

There are two main operations in this category:

Orchidectomy

This is removal of the testicles. There are two approaches that can be used. One is through the scrotum with a midline scar and the other is via the groin, which leaves two scars, similar to a hernia operation.

This operation can be combined with a scrotal skin reduction as well. It is important to remember that when the testicles have been removed, the scrotal skin will shrink / retract. This may have consequences at a later stage if a patient decides to go onto having 'full' genital reassignement surgery.

Genital Gender Reassignment

There are many different ways to perform this operation, and each surgeon will have their own approach, which may combine a combination of techniques.

In general however, whichever technique is used, the operation has three main goals:

- Creation of a clitoris
- Creation of a vaginal cavity
- Shortening and opening out of the urethra (pee tube)

Creation of Clitoris:

This is created from part of the glans (head) of the penis, on a tongue of tissue from the shaft of the penis that contains the blood vessels and nerves that supply it. The testicles are removed.

Creation of Vaginal Cavity:

The neovagina is formed by creating a space between the rectum (bowel) behind, and the bladder (in front).

The cavity is then lined with skin from the penis or scrotum, a segment / piece of bowel, or a skin graft from elsewhere, e.g. the abdomen. In most instances, bowel segments are rarely used often in the initial operation.

Laser hair removal, electrolysis or 'scraping the dermis' to remove hair follicles is performed to reduce the chances of hair growth within the cavity.

Some patients may request not to have a vaginal cavity, having a 'dimple' only at the vaginal entrance.

Shortening the Urethra:

The urethra is shortened and emerges between the vaginal cavity opening below, and the clitoris above. The urethra is often opened out as it emerges, to reduce the chances of narrowing of the opening.

2) BREAST AUGMENTATION (ENLARGEMENT)

Breast development is quite varied amongst trans women, just as it is in natal females. Breast augmentation is not recommended for at least a year after starting hormones (as per the standards of care) to allow breast growth. Often if breast growth is continuing, it may be advisable to wait until the growth plateaus before considering going ahead with surgery. There are different types of implants used (saline or silicone) and different shapes (round or tear drop / anatomical) These are placed either in front of the chest muscle (prepectoral) or behind it (subpectoral). The position is usually decided by the patient's desired look and the amount of breast tissue they have.

3) THYROID CARTILAGE / TRACHEAL / ADAM'S APPLE SHAVE:

This procedure can be done either by itself, or as is often the case, in conjunction with other surgery, especially facial feminisation surgery. It can also be performed with pitch surgery to increase the pitch of the voice. A course of speech therapy is recommended if pitch surgery is being considered.

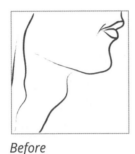 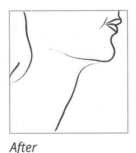

Before   *After*

4) FACIAL FEMINISATION SURGERY (FFS)

The operations in this category can be combined. The following are some of the procedures, but the list is not exhaustive:

- Hairline correction
- Hair transplants
- Forehead re-contouring
- Brow lift
- Rhinoplasty
- Cheek implants
- Lip lift
- Chin re-contouring
- Jaw re-contouring
- Fat grafting

Hairline Correction

This is performed to recreate and correct a receding hairline, and produce a more feminine appearance. It does leave a scar across the head, which can be hidden within the hairline. This is often performed in conjunction with other upper face procedures such as forehead re-contouring, and brow lift, as the same incision is used.

Hair Transplant

Can be considered for receding hair lines etc. Movement of remaining hair as part of a scalp flap procedure can also be performed. In cases of extensive baldness though, a hairpiece may be the best option.

Forehead Re-contouring

Performed to reduce the prominence of the ridge above the eye sockets, producing a more feminine contour to the forehead

Brow Lift

The female eyebrow tends to sit higher on the forehead than its male counterpart. This can be achieved either via an open procedure (combined with other forehead / hair altering procedures) or via keyhole surgery.

Cheek Augmentation

The prominence of cheeks can aesthetically enhance the appearance of both males and females. Cheek augmentation can be performed using either silicone implants or fillers.

Rhinoplasty (Nose Job)

The nose can be modified and made to appear more feminine, often by reducing the width of the nasal (alar) base, and refining the nasal tip. If the nasal skin is thick, then a significant size reduction can be achieved.

Chin Augmentation

Female chins tend to be shorter, and more pointed than male chins. Various methods are available to alter the chin via surgery (genioplasty) or use of silicone implants

Jaw Surgery

Squared angles of the mandible, and a heavier, more obvious jaw line are male characteristics. This can be achieved by increasing the bulk of the overlying masseter muscle as well as the bony contour.

B) FEMALE TO MALE SURGERY

1) CHEST SURGERY

Male and female chests are anatomically different. In females there is usually more skin, glandular tissue, and subcutaneous fat present. The nipple areolar complex (NAC) is larger and tends to be located more medially than in men. Also, females have a pronounced inframammary fold (where the breast meets the chest wall) compared to men.

The goal of surgery therefore is to remove the excess skin and glandular tissue, reduce and reposition the nipple areolar complex, and obliterate the inframammary fold with the fewest scars.

1) Peri-Areolar (Infra-areolar) Approach

Used for small breasts with a minimal amount of excess skin. Nipple position can not be changed.

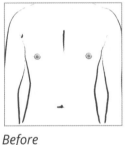 

Before   After

2) Circumareolar Approach

Used for breasts with medium amount of skin (small B maximum) or poor skin elasticity. This also allows us to move the nipple a short distance and reduce the size of the NAC.

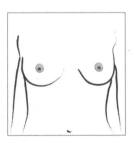 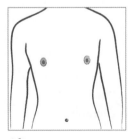

Before   After

3) Free Nipple Graft / Pedicled Nipple Flap

These techniques are used for larger breasts, and place the scar at, either the level of the nipple (see Figure 1), or at the level of the pectoralis major muscle insertion (see Figure 2).

Figure 1

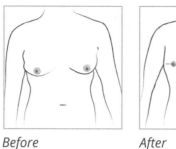
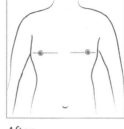

Before   *After*

Figure 2

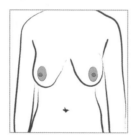
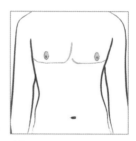

Before   *After*

2) GENITAL SURGERY

Metoidioplasty

This involves clitoral release and extending the length of the urethra so it reaches the tip of the clitoris, resulting in the creation of a micropenis. Although it is usually performed as a single procedure, it can be staged. Metoidioplasty avoids the excessive scarring and multiple procedures of a phalloplasty. The aim is to allow the patient to pee standing up.

This procedure usually requires 'priming' the clitoris with testosterone to increase the size of the glans.

It can also be combined with creation of a scrotal sac using local tissue, and insertion of testicular implants.

Phalloplasty (Creation of a Penis)

The ultimate aim is to create phallus with erogenous and tactile sensation, allowing the patient to urinate standing up, and have sexual intercourse. It is often a staged procedure involving multiple surgical specialties.

A removal of the uterus (hysterectomy) and removal of the ovaries and fallopian tubes (bilateral salpingo-opherectomy) is often performed as an initial procedure, via key-hole surgery.

Different techniques are used to produce the penile skin tube, typically using skin from the forearm, but skin from the thigh or abdomen can also be used. This is wrapped around a new extended urethra.

The clitoris is often incorporated underneath the penis, allowing for stimulation during sexual intercourse.

Skin flaps are then used to create the scrotum. Testicular implants and / or penile erection prostheses are inserted in a separate operation, often at least 12 months after the phalloplasty. Complications associated with these implants have been described, and can be quite common.

The creation of a new extended urethra means that the surgery has a higher complication rate compared with male-to-female genital surgery. As a result some surgeons will create a phallus without lengthening the urethra.

CHAPTER 15

CARE OF THE NEO-VAGINA

⚠️ **WARNING: This chapter contains graphic images of genitalia.**

 Rosemary Jones: So now the great day has come and gone, when finally, your sex affirmation surgery has been undertaken and as someone who has aspired to being a trans woman, it's a reality at last. Bruised and battered and finally overcoming the vagaries of surgery, hopefully without complications, our new woman is free to face her future and with that future comes the responsibility to maintain her neovagina in good working order. Sometimes the aftercare of the neovulva and neovagina are poorly catered for, and it may be up to the individual patient to ensure that proper care is instigated, particularly on what to do (and what not to do) with her new 'equipment'! This is a steep learning curve, which must be observed if the trans woman is to become sexually functional.

Figure 3

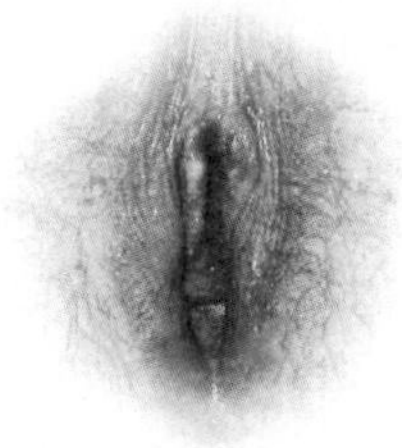

So what do you see when you look at your neovagina? Figure 3 shows the appearances of the vulva of a cis woman (born female) and Figure 4 shows the appearance of a trans woman vulva. This second picture has an appearance, which is as about as good as it ever gets. The third picture (Figure 5) shows the vulva of a longstanding trans woman, and you can see that the appearance is not as favourable as the first two pictures.

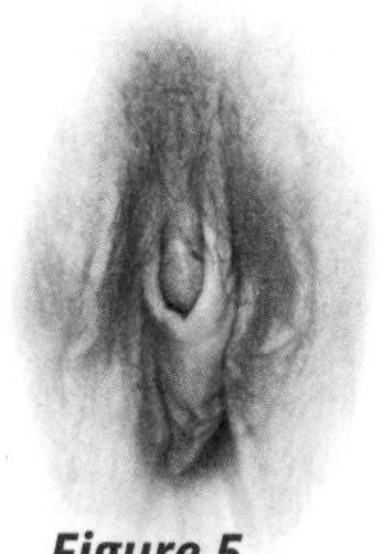

Figure 4

Figure 5

There are varying degrees of distortion in the appearance, but function may be well maintained.

Immediately postoperatively there may appear a number of problems that are mainly related to the formation of granulation tissue (healing 'proud flesh'). This is all part of the healing process and simply requires the application of silver nitrate to cauterise that tissue and allow full healing to take place comfortably. There may be bits of old suture material that can be picked out and the whole area may need to be tidied up. It is particularly important that, immediately after surgery is completed and healing proceeds, the trans woman continues to use salt water baths to keep the area clean of infection and allow good healing. One does not worry at this stage which direction the urinary stream is projected, as that will change with time, and ultimately, it is to be hoped that the urinary stream will be directed downwards into the pan, or even hit the water, as is the case in a cis woman.

Within the vagina there may be other small procedures to be undertaken by the examining doctor, and that would include cauterising granulation tissue that is otherwise invisible, but may cause bleeding when dilation is undertaken, or indeed intercourse is started. This can be distressing to the novice but is entirely harmless. You may have been supplied with a series of graded dilators, which usually come as a plastic dilator with a handle on it and are graded from one to five. Personally, I recommend the metal dildos that have a smooth, polished metal surface. These are to be preferred because, firstly, they have a graduated tip that makes entry more controllable and, secondly, the surface of the metal is smooth and engages in very little friction with the fresh vaginal skin. They have the added advantage of having a vibrator built into them if one wishes to indulge in some early experimentation. The sizes of these dilators are respectively 2.5cm and 3cm and are quite inexpensive when purchased from a shop selling sexual aids.

When initially undertaking dilation, there may be points during the procedure which cause discomfort, or even pain, as the end of the dilator catches on a ridge of skin or a ridge of scar tissue. This may need to be examined by your doctor but, generally speaking, you should continue to persevere with the dilation, with the aim of stretching that ridge of tissue so that it eventually lies back comfortably. Mostly, penetration is achieved to a depth of about 8cm to 10cm, except for those women who have been endowed with a colonic augmentation (extra piece of bowel on the top of the neovagina). 8cm to 10cm may seem too modest for some people who have been brought up on locker room mythology, where 16cm to 18cm is claimed, but this would be very much the exception rather than the rule. My opinion is that eight to 10cm is completely adequate.

It is of the greatest importance that hormonal support is established fairly early. It is clear that the cis woman's vulva requires testosterone cream as a topical application, and, of course, the vagina requires oestrogen cream. One might ask whether a trans woman's neovaginal skin should be treated with oestrogen or with testosterone, given that the skin of origin comes from the penis, which would be testosterone dependent skin. In some informal investigations that I undertook many years ago, there was a suggestion that the hormonal receptivity of the neovaginal skin changes from that of testosterone exclusively, to a mixture of oestrogen and testosterone reception. It follows from this that it can be entirely acceptable to use an oestrogen cream within the neovagina, as would be the case in a cis woman with a naturally born vagina. I am encouraged then to give an oestrogen cream or tablet to a trans woman to put in her vagina, perhaps daily to begin with, and then on to perhaps three times a week in subsequent months. When dilating, I encourage them to put some oestrogen cream on the dilator as a lubricant. The oestrogen cream has the effect of softening the vaginal skin so that it's more readily amenable to being stretched, whether by dilator or by penis. It is true to say that oestrogen cream does not get absorbed very much once the skin of the vagina becomes modified by the oestrogen. Most trans women are reluctant to use testosterone cream on their neovulva, just as a cis woman might. When it is applied to the vulva, or indeed elsewhere, testosterone cream is very well absorbed, and this may not be to the liking of the neophyte trans woman, being the 'hated hormone'. So, if the skin around the neovulva becomes sore, salt bathing is recommended, with the added possibility of occasional steroid cream as an alternate to testosterone cream. Testosterone cream may also be tried if the trans woman experiences recurrent cystitis or voiding difficulties thought to be associated with the urethra.

The ultimate fate of the neovagina in terms of function relies exclusively on whether that vagina is used sexually. Interestingly, I have found that neovaginas that have been subjected to penile intercourse are in very much better shape in terms of compliance, compared to those in which dilation only (or indeed no dilation at all) has been used. That doesn't mean to say that the latter women are second-class citizens. Indeed, there may be many of us who have a neovagina created but we remain virgins. That, after all, is the fate of some cis women, and may be entirely in accord with their wishes.

While it remains true to say that the success of the neovagina is largely dependent on the skill of the surgeon creating that equipment, there are problems that can occur irrespective of how well the procedure is carried out. The technique of sex affirmation surgery has improved greatly over previous decades. In saying this, I am referring here mainly to the so-called penile inversion technique, where the skin of the neovagina is lined by penile skin. In some centres, scrotal skin may be used, but that carries with it the hazard of hair growing within the vagina that can be very unpleasant, certainly in the case that I examined. The technique of colonic augmentation (extending the length and size of the vagina using a loop of bowel) is not favoured so much these days, as there are a number of problems that can arise.

A characteristic error, at least in previous surgeries, is that of leaving in too much residual erectile tissue (residual corpus cavernosum). The rested appearance is shown in Figure 6 and when that woman strained downwards (Figure 7) you can see the bulge of this residual erectile tissue.

Figure 6

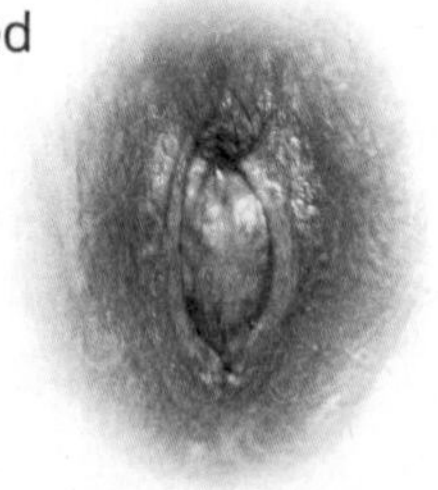

Figure 7

Or, in Figure 8, you can see that erectile tissue bulging forwards in a woman who had brought herself to complete arousal. This can be problematical to the woman when she is making love, as the tissue may obstruct the entry of the penis. It may also be a problem when a woman becomes inappropriately aroused, and as a result, finds walking difficult. This residual erectile tissue is capable of being surgically excised but that procedure has to be done with considerable care to ensure that the pipe to the bladder (the urethra) is not damaged. The other risk of excision of this residual tissue is that the most sensitively erotogenic area of the neovagina, being at, or near the G-spot of a cis woman, may be damaged and compromise future ability to become aroused. In Figure 9, you can see the same woman when she is not aroused and the various components of her lower vagina, including progressive damage of the skin shown as 'dehiscing skin'. In Figure 10, you can see the result of the repair work three days postoperatively, that shows every sign of a return to normality.

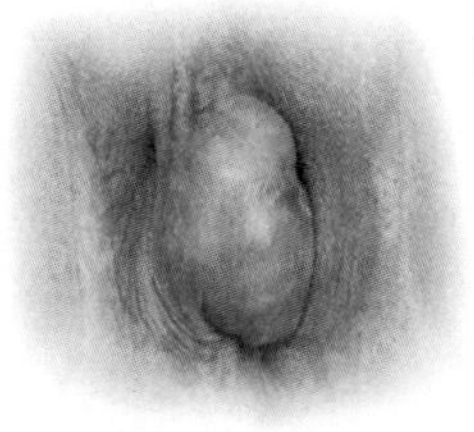

Figure 8

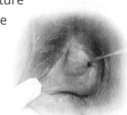

Figure 9

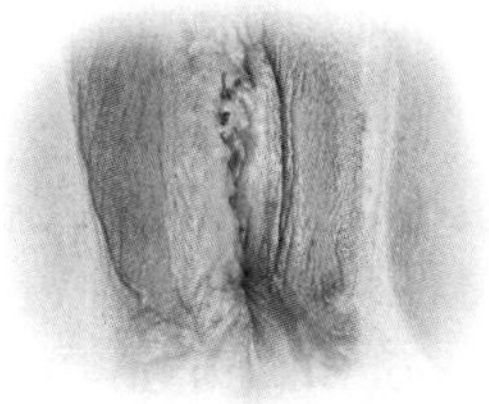

A further problem may be that the appearances of the labia majora (the lips of the vagina) may be not full and rounded, as they would be in a cis woman. Not many individuals actually complain about this but, to my eye, the appearance can be less than satisfactory, and I wonder at times whether a competent plastic surgeon might consider filling out those lips with a fat transplant.

Figure 10

In Figure 11 you can see the long term complication of prolapse of the neovagina. This is basically an extrusion of the neovagina and the neovaginal skin outside the neovulva. For whatever reason, the suspension of the neovagina has broken away from its moorings. You can see how very unsatisfactory this appearance is, at least in the operating theatre. I treated this particular individual with an innovative procedure called a laparoscopic

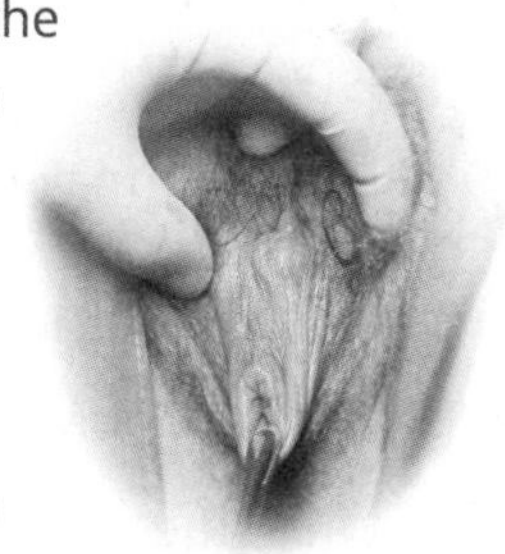

Figure 11

resuspension of the neovagina, and the result of that intervention is shown in Figure 12 .

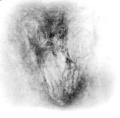

Then there is the interesting question of the 'micro environment' of the neovagina and how that compares to that of the cis woman. The well-oestrogenised cis vagina contains little bugs that are capable of converting the glycogen in the skin of the vagina to a weak acid which keeps the

Figure 12

vaginal skin clean and healthy The woman with a neovagina does not have the capacity to produce glycogen and doesn't have the natural inheritance of these friendly little bugs. So there is more work to do with the neovagina than there is with the natural vagina, and the use of acidifying creams, such as Aci-Jel, is encouraged. In addition to Aci-Jel, I often slip a Probiotic capsule into the end of the oestrogen cream applicator and that does carry some of the natural bugs that exist in the vagina and in the bowel. Whether this has any added advantage is uncertain but in at least one severely compromised individual, it had the desired effect of overcoming heavy secondary infection and an offensive discharge. So a combination of an oestrogen cream, Aci-Jel or similar, plus Probiotic seems to be the recipe for achieving a comfortable and clean smelling organ.

Perhaps a word about lubricants is in order. It is best to use a thoroughly reliable liquid Silk type of lubricant that is smooth, effective and disperses easily. One needs to avoid is putting oily substances in the neovagina, or indeed the natural vagina, since those oily substances may obstruct the entrance of the vagina, which always needs to be able to 'breathe'. If the neck of the vagina becomes obstructed by oil or similar, there may be a stagnation of substances within the neovagina that degrade and give that offensive odour that is very easily recognised by most women.

Douching may be useful in evacuating old, dead cellular material, remnants of semen, and other material. I would say however, that obsessive douching of the neovagina is probably a mistake and should probably be only undertaken every fortnight or so.

While the appearances of the cis vagina and the neovagina and their respective vulvas may be very similar, their function may be entirely different. Arousal in a cis woman is mainly via the clitoris and that, no matter what the surgeons may say, is usually absent in a functional sense in the neovulva. The neoclitoris is a 'window dressing' organ. The usual site of erotic arousal in the trans woman is around the skin at the entrance to the neovagina or just within the vagina at the point where the urethra meets the bladder or, as the cis woman knows, the G-spot. Most of the younger trans women seem to be able to achieve an orgasm and sometimes very successfully so. Perhaps in the older trans woman, with more recently installed 'apparatus,' that may not be so obviously the case. It is a function worth pursuing however, as the rewards are very great for persistent effort.

CHAPTER 16

BEING TRANS, LIVING TRANS – A PERSONAL ACCOUNT

Melissa Vick: **What is it like being trans? What is it like living as a trans person?**

There are three obvious answers: it's largely the same as living as a non-trans ('cisgender') person; conversely, it's different from living as a cisgender person; and, it's different for each of us.

In this chapter, I'll unpack some of the evidence for each of these answers. I'll draw on my own experience, and my knowledge of the experiences of many more trans people, both from my extended trans social network, and more formally, from an open-ended research project documenting transition experiences, especially of young adult trans women.

How is being trans the same as living as a cis person?

We still have all the everyday demands and routines of life to deal with. We have to make some form of living (study, work, or social security). We have to deal with all sorts of other people: shop assistants, bus drivers, doctors, colleagues, lovers, friends, and family. We still have to deal with other institutions and government agencies. And of course, we have to secure our basic material needs of food and shelter; we have to pay the rent, buy our groceries, and do the dishes. But to a large extent, the way these everyday issues present themselves to us is different from the way cisgender people encounter them.

For me, for instance, transitioning at work, where I was head of my department at the university where I had been employed for 23 years, meant 'outing' myself selectively for the first six months. First, to selected colleagues, including my own manager, and later, to colleagues, students, and my international academic networks.

Transitioning also meant telling my parents – who for 62 years had known me as their son – that I wasn't their son anymore. I was dreading their rejection and the hurt, and I understood the sense of loss they were likely to feel.

I have also had to judge whether, when, and how to tell potential lovers. And then there were the administrators and competitors in my newly adopted sport of table tennis when I wanted to enter regional, state, and national competitions.

How is being trans different from living as a cis person?

We (trans people) have all sorts of personal issues to deal with that are different from, and may be over and above, issues that cis people deal with. While cis people and trans people alike have to deal with everyday issues of health (common seasonal issues and accidental injuries), trans people also have to deal with issues related to the hormone regimes that are central to many of our lives. This includes regular monitoring, and potential long-term flow-on effects, such as the impact on our livers.

Trans men, unlike cis men, characteristically have to deal with gynaecological health. While both cis and trans women (but also men) are vulnerable to breast cancer, trans women may have to deal with risks of prostate cancer that cannot affect other women. For me, this has also meant having to explain to my doctor why I haven't had a cervical smear, and why I have needed a prostate check. It's meant explaining to the nurse at the breast screening clinic why I hadn't had a mammogram until the age of 64, and telling the receptionist why my gender marker was M for male when I visited the hospital Emergency Department with a sprained ankle. None of these are big issues, but each one is potentially awkward, and could lead to discrimination and transphobic reactions.

Other 'personal' issues arise from the different relationships we have with our life histories: how do we relate to the person we lived as for however many years it was before we recognised ourselves as trans?

Am I still the same person? And if I'm not, what is the relationship between the 'other' self and 'me'? How do I deal with that, in terms of the continuity of my life?

Many of us never quite felt 'right' as the boy or man, girl or woman we had always been identified as, and have long felt that the way our culture orders and understands gender doesn't really match our reality. We have struggled, and continue to struggle, to create a better sense of ourselves and our gender, and to have others appreciate how awkward that makes it to move comfortably in our society. In addition, many of us are also dealing with a powerful heritage of tensions around our sense of self, and the relations between our 'selves' and our 'bodies' that continues to trouble us. For me, it has taken seven years of transition to get past the easily-triggered moments of deep sobbing grief over the sense that someone else lived my life, and that my own life as Melissa was a deep, dark void.

All categories of people are subject to violence and may be subject to prejudice of various sorts. Cis and trans people of colour are likely to encounter racism. Cis and trans people with a range of physical disabilities encounter a social world in which they are commonly seen as somehow inferior; in which they are rendered objects of pity or contempt. They also encounter a material world largely built on the assumption that people are able bodied and, by neglect and oversight, are forced to face challenges that life does not present others. Cis and trans people who are gay are likely to experience homophobia.

Trans people are also subject to prejudice and discrimination on the basis of our gender. The effects of multiple dimensions of prejudice commonly compound each other to make the world a far riskier place than it is for the cis people, with whom we share other attributes.

Our lives also differ from those of cis people in that we have to negotiate a world in which it is assumed that there are only two types of people (male and female). That our sex and gender are determined by nature, enshrined in our chromosomes, and revealed by our genitalia and are necessarily and unalterably the same. This overwhelmingly common way of seeing the world – which many now call cisnormativity – makes us appear to many (and may even lead us to feel) like oddities at best, and at worst, freaks.

The associated prejudice, which we call cissexism, works socially to make trans people more commonly subject to violence and discrimination than our cis 'equivalents'. As a population, we are poorer, more socially marginalised, have poorer health, are less educated, less employed, more bullied, more imprisoned, and more subject to violence of various sorts, from harassment and bullying to bashings and murder.

While generally, I feel quite secure – there's lots of evidence that I 'pass', that I'm rarely seen as 'a man in a dress' or a 'tranny' – those moments where I know I have been 'picked' instantly raise my levels of fear and anxiety for my physical safety, sometimes to panic level.

It is perhaps worth mentioning here, though, that for many of us, encountering or coming to terms with what we may describe as our 'true' selves can be transformative. The sense of unbridled liberation can infuse our lives with a richness and joy that might be likened to the experience that some people describe when they undergo a life-changing spiritual or religious encounter – a sense of being 'born again'. One of my closest friends described my mood for about the first year of my transition as 'nauseatingly euphoric', and my mother has repeatedly said that she takes consolation for the loss of her son from the fact that she sees me being happy in ways she never saw before.

Thus far, I have talked about the similarities and the differences between cis people and trans people. But we know that cis people differ dramatically from one another. While they may share broad characteristics that come from their genders, their social class, their levels of affluence or poverty, their region or nationality, people still differ within such categories. They also differ in more individual ways, e.g. temperament, styles of interactions, leisure preferences, physical and mental health, and sense of wellbeing. The same is true for trans people. It is true that, for each aspect of life that we share with cis people – we vary by class, race, gender, education and so on. I am acutely aware of how much easier my own transition was than many of my friends' transitions because of my generally supportive work environment, family and friendship network, and by the fact that I was in a secure, well-paid occupation.

We also differ enormously in aspects of our experience directly related to our 'trans-ness'. One dimension of this is the age at which we recognise that we are trans, and at which we decide to undertake transition. There are clearly very significant differences between experiences. On the one hand, there are those who recognise themselves as different from the gender we were assigned at birth, and have parental support, from early childhood. On the other hand, there are those of us who struggle with puberty in a gender we are not comfortable in, and those of us who struggle with an unnamed or misnamed set of issues, e.g. guilt as a closet cross-dressing sissy, or the self-hatred that comes from living a life with marriages and families before recognising 'the problem' or coming to terms with what we've struggled against for so long. I was unaware that I was trans until I was 62, and my recognition of that fact came in a moment of epiphany. I simply realised who I was. I knew why I had felt so deeply troubled my entire life. And yet, in retrospect, I can see there were some staggeringly obvious pointers from when I was 11, and then, even more so, when I was about 30. At the time, I misrecognised them as signs of perversion. I thought I was burdened with an imagination and desires that would send me to hell, and I experienced all the guilt that came with those realisations.

We differ in the ease or difficulty of our struggle to accept our trans-ness, and in our strategies for dealing with, or managing our transitions, and our life as trans people. For some of us, the lack of self-confidence, depression, and other accompaniments of living at odds with ourselves, as well as the potential costs – like the fear that we will lose our loved ones – make it almost impossible even to imagine that we might ever undertake transition. And, as a result, we stay feeling trapped and helpless. For many of us who do transition, those fears become reality; many of us lose our parents, siblings, partners, children, and friends, as well as our jobs. In some cases, family dissolution brings with it legal and financial stresses.

As we begin transition, for various reasons, including difficulties in finding or affording quality medical services many of us opt to self-medicate rather than what many trans people experience as jumping through the hoops required by health services. Another crucial choice we make is whether to:

• Adopt a 'stealth' transition (in which we create an essentially new life for ourselves in which we appear as cis people in the gender with which we identify).

- Transition openly, but without focusing on our trans-ness, but rather on the other aspects of our lives that have not changed, such as our workplace expertise.

- Adopt an 'activist' or 'out and proud' stance in which we use our trans status to draw attention to the misrepresentations and misunderstandings of trans-ness that saturate our culture, and seek to redress the discriminations we face.

Such decisions may change as we become more settled in our new lives and genders. Certainly, I've settled comfortably into my new life and sense of myself. I have, once again, become more engaged in other concerns than 'trans issues', and my network of friends has become less dominated by trans men and women. Nonetheless, I live with a double identity: I am a woman, and I am a trans woman. And I continue to be involved in my own form of trans activism.

We have different goals for the transformations of our bodies. Not only are there significant differences between trans men's options and trans women's options but, regardless of medical technology, many younger trans women appear to be embracing themselves as women with penises, and have no plans for genital surgery. Our medical and body-related strategies may also relate to differences in social position, background and opportunity - such as the interplays between age, education, class, racial / ethnic / cultural background and employment. Related to this we have varied concerns with 'passing'. Some of us seek to assimilate invisibility as members of our 'new' gender, others contest the various norms of gender presentation in varying degrees (e.g. trans women who choose to maintain a 'masculine' voice, or opt for 'gender-queer' presentations that clearly challenge identification with either of the 'normal' binary alternatives).

We differ widely in our sexualities, both our orientations (hetero, homo, bi, pan) and sexual practices. Inevitably, the sexual histories we inherit – especially those of us with 'late' transitions – interact with our trans lives. Many of us maintain our preference for the same bodies we always preferred, although some of us discover new pleasures with differently sexed partners. Those of us whose long-term partners leave might experience living alone, perhaps for the first time in our adult lives, struggling to find lovers who accept us and our bodies, dealing with rejection and loneliness. And those of us battling long histories of self-loathing and an avoidance of intimacy may struggle to form the various types of romantic, sexual, emotional, and domestic relationships we now desire. Many of us have sexual histories strongly marked by fetishism. For example, pre-transition, trans women often engage in forced feminisation, and that tends to be associated with submissiveness and masochism. (My own involvement in forced feminisation was one of the things that allowed me to think I was 'just kinky' rather than to recognise that I was trans). Post transition, while some of our roles and practices may change (from submissive to dominant, or from masochist to sadist, and our need for forced feminisation may simply dissolve), our well-developed fetishistic practices and networks often remain as integral and ongoing elements in our lives.

Finally, for some of us, transition is the key to resolving many, if not most, of the 'personal issues' that troubled us. For many, however, a range of issues that may be directly, indirectly related, or even unrelated, to our trans-ness, continue, ranging from depression, through drug addictions, to incomplete education, unemployment, and poverty. I consider myself to have been fortunate: transition, and the self-acceptance it was based on, did resolve a host of personal troubles. And yet, I still retain some old habits, especially in close relationships, that, apparently, have nothing to do with my being trans, and that continue to give grief to those who allow themselves to be close to me.

For those who share our lives, and wish to understand and support us, it is crucial to recognise both the range of issues that might come along with our trans-ness. Equally, it is important to recognise and understand the idiosyncratic way these common issues play through our individual lives. None of us conforms to any of the stereotypes of us that can be found in the literature and the mass media. In view of that, it is important to make all our voices heard. We should set our own directions and priorities, and work through our issues as we think best.

CHAPTER 17

YOUNG AND TRANSGENDER

Luka Griffin: Teenagers are stereotyped as lazy, angsty, horrible messes of children. Stuck in that awkward stage between child and adult, life can be hard. School, dating, formal assessments, and the added stresses of finding out who you are, and what you want to do is tough. But what about being a transgender teenager?

I came out as a transgender man at the young age of 14 years old. I spent most of my late childhood and early teens contemplating my concept of self: ranging from my gender, of course, all the way to, strangely, my favourite colour. Your teens are a time of massive change, some good, some bad. For a transgender teen, going through puberty was like going through hell. I hated having no control over the changes happening to my body, and how, mostly, I had no control over how people perceived my body.

One of my earliest memories is lying in bed at night, praying to God to make me a boy. I was six years old. My religious education teacher had made it clear that if you ask God for something, he delivers. But I woke up the next morning, utterly confused. Nothing had changed.

Through the years leading to teenage-hood, I had endured the questions of 'Are you a boy or a girl?' I do believe one of the reasons these questions never seemed to stop was because I never gave them a straight answer. Simply put, I didn't know the answer!

I had loved my style of dress: extremely masculine, with short hair, and always playing stereotypical boys games. I felt happy and content being perceived as a boy. But of course, the source of everyone's confusion (and what seemed my own) was the fact that my family and friends continuously referred to me as a girl. I accepted the common discomforts of being called a girl, but never enjoyed it. More than once, I wondered if everyone felt like I did, confused about a core part of their sense of self.

As I went into teenagehood, the discomfort became unbearable as people stopped asking if I was a boy or a girl. My body was changing – and it only reinforced their perception of me as female. I couldn't control people's perceptions of my body, and I felt defeated. It had been easier for me to ignore my own internal gender confusion when everyone else seemed to be confused about it too. But my body was changing, and the discomfort was too much. I didn't feel like I could ignore those feelings any more. I didn't want to keep trying to be something I wasn't.

I needed to understand why I felt the way I did. Fortunately, YouTube and the internet came to the rescue, with multiple resources ranging from 'How I knew I was trans' to 'Quiz: are you trans?' I found a YouTube video called, 'How I knew I was transgender (and some advice on coming out)' by Skylar Kergil, a transgender man and activist. The video talked about his experience of finding out and accepting that he was transgender. He explained how, before his transition, he felt there were parts of his body that didn't match his idea of himself. This idea really connected with me. He talked about how he tried for a long time to ignore those feelings, how he acted a certain way and pretended to be someone else. He said that he thought cutting his hair short and wearing masculine clothes might be enough to make him feel better about himself, but it wasn't. He was saying all the things that, as an 11-year-old I had been thinking and feeling.

I felt so much relief. Because somebody actually knew how I was feeling, it helped give me a new understanding of myself. Some of the confusion, frustration, and anxiety was easier to deal with, just knowing there were other people in the world who felt like me.

It was like a light had been turned on in my mind. I knew I was a transgender man, and I knew that I didn't want to be called by my birth name. But I was also scared. I didn't know what to do. How would people treat me if they found out who I was? I was worried about what this new understanding meant for my life. And I was scared of how my parents would react. But finding out more about what transgender was online, and knowing of transgender people on the internet gave me the strength in myself to think about how to tell my family and friends. I remember bringing up some examples of trans men in conversations with mum, saying I'd watched a video and it was really interesting, just to see what Mum's reaction would be. To see if she would accept me.

After building up all my courage, one night, I asked my mother to come into my room. I sat her down and before I could start talking, I started crying. I was so scared and worried that she would hate me that I was overwhelmed. The only words I could get out were, 'Mum … I … I think I'm …' and she said, 'You think you're trans, don't you?' I just nodded. She hugged me and said, 'Oh baby, I love you. We'll figure it out.'

With my dad, I emailed him a letter explaining what being trans was, and telling him that I was trans. Unlike Mum, my dad had never had any deep interactions with transgender people, but he texted me to let me know he loved me and wanted to talk about what we needed to do from here.

Although I don't want to romanticise my experience, I was lucky. I had a fairy-tale response from my parents, family, and friends. Unconditional love is such a powerful thing. Even if I'm trans, I'm still worthy of love, whether it's romantic love, love of myself, or love from my parents. Sometimes being trans is hard, but it doesn't change the fact that I'm still a human being. The most courageous thing I can do as a trans person is love myself.

From that point on, my experience of being a teenager changed. Before coming out, I knew I was a man. I knew I was transgender, but I was never treated as such. Once the public began to see me as a transgender man, the reality set in that my trans identity was the most prominent and notable aspect of my being. Teenage life became different once I came out as trans.

One of the most significant differences was that my life became dictated by the medical and legal systems. Because I knew that, at 13 years old, I needed to go on testosterone, I was required to engage with processes that were out of my control.

My mother took me for my first ever appointment with the gender specialist at the local Sexual Health Clinic at 14. In that first 45-minute meeting, I was told that because I was a transgender teenager, I would have to go through a series of appointments with different types of doctors, just to decide I was transgender. I was confused. I had already told them I was transgender. Why did they question it?

This treatment and examination by medical institutions is just a routine part of life for transgender teens. While for me, there was never any question that I was trans, the medical involvement ensured that others trusted my judgement. In Australia, unlike many other countries, a transgender person under the age of 18, is unable to access testosterone without going to Family Court for legal approval.

The Family Court required that I was diagnosed with gender dysphoria, and that it was confirmed by multiple doctors, all specialising in gender. They confirmed that I was competent enough to know what going on testosterone meant. It can be easier to manage the family Court process in major capital cities, where the hospitals are experienced in supporting young transgender people in getting necessary treatment. But being in rural Australia, I was the first person in my city to take my case to court. This was only possible through the assistance of pro bono solicitors and a barrister from a capital city who dedicated their time to my case. They knew how important the process was to me, and wanted me to go on testosterone as much as I wanted to go on testosterone.

Every person in the courtroom that day – the solicitors, the barrister, the child safety representative, my parents, me, my family and friends, and the judge – all agreed that not only was I Gillick competent (meaning I could consent to testosterone treatment for myself), but also that the Family Court process itself was unjust, unnecessary, and, ultimately, pointless. I began testosterone treatment ten days later.

I think that my success in the Family Court and going on testosterone enabled me to walk through life with a confidence I had never experienced before. It felt like the weight of gender dysphoria had reduced to a more manageable level.

I began a series of regular visits to a gender psychologist, and paediatric endocrinologists. I travelled 1340km to see a paediatric gender dysphoria psychiatrist. There were home visits from nurses for hormone blocker injections, and regular visits to general medical practitioners. And I made fortnightly visits to the Sexual Health Clinic for gender counselling and hormone injections. I can't remember the time when I walked into the clinic and had to say my name and why I was there to the staff. Now I know the staff by name, they know me, and why I'm there. The sexual health clinic is almost my second home. To continuously go to a single place that isn't school, at least every month from the time I was 14 to even now, is almost ridiculous.

After starting on testosterone, I moved into distance education. I now needed to present as male while I was at school, as well as in my home life. The school I went to was extremely accommodating regarding uniform choice. They had a policy of supporting and accepting students who experienced gender dysphoria and were transitioning, which included wearing the most comfortable uniform and using the preferred bathroom.

The Principal had done a lot of research into how to accept a trans student, and was really open to listening to my point of view. I'll always be grateful for that. I chose the men's uniform at school, and was pleasantly surprised at the impact this had on the quality of my school experience. When I was going through the family court process and home school, people saw me as a trans man, not just as a man. Going to school and being able to put on that uniform meant I was not singled out as a trans man, I was included as a man in wider society for the first time.

I am not ashamed of being trans, and I love my trans identity, but never before had I been so validated as a man in the gender binary.

Though being recognised as a man by wider society is an affirming experience, it has never been vital to me identifying as a man. My decision to pursue testosterone was for myself, so that my gender dysphoria could be alleviated. It was not so that other people would position me as a man. When I first learnt about going on testosterone (at 11-years-old) and I first found out what trans was, I thought that to be trans, you had to medically transition. That being trans meant wanting to be cis. But as I grew, and my understanding of being trans evolved, I then realised that my desire to medically transition had never been about anybody else, or what other people would think of me, or how they would position me. It was always so I could feel more content in my physical sense of self.

As a young transgender person, I am so grateful to the previous generations of transgender men and women who have continuously advocated for the rights and opportunities we now enjoy as transgender teenagers. Being a trans teenager is still not easy. There is the ever-present difficulty in medical transitioning, the struggle of the legal process, and the stress of being a teenager in general. But if you had asked me what I wanted to do at 14-years-old, I would've said 'Go on testosterone'. Now that I have accomplished that, I want to enable more teenagers like me to access the hormones they need without unnecessary barriers that create further anxiety. Whether this means becoming a solicitor and fighting for trans kids on a pro bono basis, or becoming a politician and abolishing the Family Court process and develop something more effective and respectful for trans youth and their families, I'm still figuring that out. Just like every other teenager, I have lots of hope for the future.

CHAPTER 18

WHAT DO WE TELL THE CHILDREN?

Az Hakeem: Before you think about what you tell the children, what have you told yourself? This is the bit you need to be clear about before you tell your children anything. The next thing you need to bear in mind is the developmental stage of the child. You'll need to be aware of the limits of their understanding and try not to overload or overwhelm them.

Sometimes, a person who is in a state of flux or confusion with regards their sense of gender identity, who has a close relationship with their young children, might be keen to share their thoughts of changing gender – about how 'Daddy' might want to be a 'Mummy'. I usually advise my patients to hold off until they are more certain in their own mind of any decisions about their gender identity, including whether they are going to pursue any physical sex or gender role changes.

People going through a period of experimentation with clothing and gender roles who also live with young children, have often described to me how they chose to do it once their children had gone to bed, to prevent having to engage in complicated explanations as to their unfamiliar appearance. They commonly described the worry as to what they would say to their children if they were to see them or find their 'secret clothes'. My advice is that whilst the experimentation with the gendered appearance may be a big deal for them, it was not necessary to convey the '*big deal*' to their children in the early stages. Upon discovery of '*daddy in a dress*', rather than nervously blurting out a panicky confession of gender dysphoria and contemplation of a future sex-change to a bewildered five-year-old, it is probably best to keep things simple, and on a level which they could understand. Young children understand concepts of dressing up and fancy-dress outfits, so one simple emergency explanation to have at hand for parents is along the lines of, *'Sometimes Daddy finds it fun dressing up in fancy-dress, just like you do'* which is often all that is needed, and is usually well received.

Vignette: Vincent

Vincent lived with his partner and their two children. Vincent came out to his partner last year as having gender dysphoria, and wishing to spend some time experimenting dressing and presenting himself in a female gender role. He is not sure whether he will eventually take things further or consider physical gender reassignment options in the future and has not yet seen anyone at the gender clinic. Prior to coming out to his partner, Vincent would 'cross-dress' in his partner's clothes and use her make-up when she was out. But he plucked up the courage to have 'the conversation' with her last year. Since then, his wife has supported him cross-dressing in the evenings when their children have gone to bed, albeit not in her clothes but items he has purchased for his own use. It was a struggle for Vincent's partner to understand why Vincent wanted to cross-dress and they both feel it would be difficult for their children to get their heads around it as they were only three and five-years-old.

One evening, after the kids had gone to bed, a cross-dressed Vincent and his wife were in the kitchen having a glass of wine together, and the five-year-old son entered the room having not been able to get to sleep. The son was shocked to see Daddy in a dress but Vincent and his wife told their son that they were having a fancy-dress game where Daddy was letting Mummy dress him up like Mummy for a bit of fancy-dress fun as a forfeit for not doing the washing up properly. They smiled and laughed together and asked their son whether Daddy 'looked funny dressed up like Mummy'. Their son entered into the spirit of what was proposed to be the situation, and his initial shock turned into gaiety. Later, he was able to return to bed laughing at his parents' funny game. Years later, when their son was older, Vincent and his partner were able to talk to their son about that night as a way of beginning to explain Vincent's gender dysphoria, and his wish to live full time in a trans female role, which, by that time, he had decided he wished to pursue.

Parents contemplating gender reassignment understandably worry as to when is the best time to tell their children, and whether this would have a damaging impact on them. Sometimes, as with other decisions affecting parenting, such as parental divorce or separation, the parents may choose to wait until their children are above a certain age in order to go ahead, as their children may be more likely to understand. Of course, there are no clear rules and there is no 'good time', and professionals are unlikely to advise waiting until the children reach a specific age. Common sense would advise against introducing any kind of major situation for children to adjust to (such as moving house / school / emigrating / parent transitioning) at a time when they may need to focus on crucial exams and many parents take such timings into consideration in such cases. The pros and cons of when to tell one's children or when to choose to transition are for the individual to weigh up with consideration of the specifics of their situation, taking into consideration their own needs and wishes regarding gender transition, as well as the impact upon any parental relationship and their children. There is no evidence indicating what the impact of parents undergoing gender transition is upon children of differing ages, and as such, there is no evidence-based guidance on the best time, or least disruptive time (and it would be very difficult to conduct such a study). Generally, children are quite resilient and often less shocked than the parents may anticipate. These days children are more aware than ever of terms such as 'transgender', and teenagers especially seem very familiar with examples of post-transition transgender persons from the world of celebrity and social media.

If a parent is planning on undergoing gender reassignment then it would be helpful for the children to have access to someone other than the transitioning parent whom they can talk to openly about their thoughts, curiosities, and any fears, in a safe and confidential environment. This does not necessarily need to be a formal therapeutic setting, but the availability of an understanding grandparent, aunt, uncle, teacher or similar consistent figure who is available, willing, and able to provide this function would be a great help to the child. The person doesn't need to be an expert in gender dysphoria themselves; their function would be to help the child process their own emotional responses to the transition as a reassuring sounding board, with whom the child feels they can talk safely.

Once a definite decision has been made regarding parental gender transition, it is advisable for parents to inform the children's school so that they are made aware of any considerations regarding the period of adjustment for the child, and any additional support the child may need. Aspects to take into consideration around this time include helping the child come to terms with what's happening. The effects of this period of adjustment may be reflected in their schoolwork so it should be taken into consideration by the school, and they should also be alert to the possibility of any adverse reactions from other children in the playground, or indeed the parents from the other children in the school.

Children are used to taking in new and novel experiences, more so than adults in many ways. As most parents will know, children often take cues from adults in terms of how to emotionally experience an event. When their toddler falls and grazes their knee, an overly anxious parent who responds to their grazed toddler as if a catastrophe has occurred will probably induce a terrified response in the toddler, whose emotional processing is strongly moulded by emotional cues from their environment. On the other hand, the parent who responds in a comforting and calm manner, smiles and indicates that although the graze might hurt, it is not the end of the world, so the brave toddler need not worry, will find themselves with an infant who is far less distressed by their grazed knee. So why am I rambling on about infants with grazed knees? The point here is how children take cues for emotionally processing events from their environment, especially from the emotional tone of the adult conveying the situation to them. While gender transition may be a big, complex and at times uncertain, or even daunting, series of changes for the adult involved, these emotions do not need to be conveyed to the child. The information should ideally be conveyed in a calm, non-dramatic manner, in a comfortable environment by those with whom the child feels safe with. The children should have time to process how they feel about what they have understood. They should have access to someone they trust so they are sufficiently comfortable enough to ask all the frank, enquiring, politically-incorrect, and difficult questions which children would be expected to ask when getting their heads around something new.

CHAPTER 19

'I CHANGED MY SEX,
THEN CHANGED MY MIND!'

Az Hakeem: Whilst sex-reassignment is a useful intervention for many with a fixed cross-sexed binary gender identity (with realistic expectations and awareness of the limitations of surgery) it is by no means a one-size-fits-all solution. That's why gender clinics offer a careful screening process. Despite this, approximately a quarter of the people referred to my specialist gender dysphoria psychotherapy service, over a ten-year period, had previously undergone physical sex-reassignment, but were still experiencing gender dysphoria. They were referred for psychotherapy – still confused and unhappy about their sense of gender – but now with a post-operative sex-changed body which they had no wish for, doubling their sense of identity confusion. The proportion of post-op 'regretters' who had been assessed by my gender dysphoria psychotherapy service was around one in four.

Clearly this is far higher than the prevalence of post-operative regretters in the general population. But the sample I looked at was very skewed as the population was restricted to those people who had been referred to a gender dysphoria psychotherapy service.

Most of the 'regretters' gave a history of believing that sex-reassignment was *'the only treatment'* for gender identity conditions, either from their own research or from the advice of their general practice doctor or psychiatrist. Some had gone through the specialist gender clinics, having researched the *'correct answers'* in order to progress past the perceived *'gatekeepers'* blocking them from hormones and surgery. Others had bypassed the gender clinic and flown to surgeons abroad for gender reassignment without a 'real-life test' or trial of living full time in their desired gender role, and without receiving any hormones first.

Vignette: Adam

Adam had spent many years having sexualised fantasies of having a vagina, and as such, researched online and came to the conclusion that he must be transgender. His research led him to believe that physical gender reassignment would be the solution to his predicament. Adam had had a religious upbringing and still identified strongly with his particular faith. He decided against seeking specialist help from a gender identity clinic due to the long waiting list, and a wish to sort the problem out quickly by accessing the treatments he had read about online which he believed were right for him. He wasn't sure about the usual recommendation of living in the female role prior to taking hormones before sex-reassignnment surgery, as he felt that this was 'not the way in which God made women'. Adam believed that girls were born first with their vagina, prior to then developing breasts during the hormonal changes in puberty, and then lived in the adult female role. As such, Adam believed that the correct way for him would be to get a vagina first, and then take hormones and to live in the female gender role once he had done this.

Adam booked a flight overseas and arranged for a surgeon to perform a vaginoplasty with a view to returning home to commence cross-sex hormones and live in the female gender role. If Adam had undergone a thorough assessment from a gender clinic specialist they would have been able to advise Adam that his sexual excitement in relation to his fantasy of having a vagina was due to autogynaephilia rather than transgender, and they would have warned against the consequent problems of him undergoing sex-reassignment surgery. Adam awoke from the surgery and was immediately filled with post-operative regret. The vaginoplasty operation had of course involved a full castration, and consequently, he experienced a marked loss of libido and the end of his previous sexual fantasies of having a vagina. Adam realised that his gender identity was not that of being female and he had no wish to have the neo-vagina which he now had.

Adam flew back home and developed a severe reactive depression. He was referred to a gender clinic, and they referred him to me for specialist psychotherapy. Adam continued to live in the male gender role and refused to look at or touch his neo-vagina or attend to the necessary post-operative care procedures required. As a result, his severe depression was compounded by also having to endure the physical problems of poor wound healing, surgical adhesions, and infection associated with failing to attend to the post-operative healing process. Adam was filled with a sense of shame, regret and despair and a fear that those around him would know the secret he was hiding. He felt unable to discuss it with anyone he knew, which further reinforced his sense of isolation and despair.

I saw Adam for individual psychotherapy initially, before introducing him into one of my weekly gender dysphoria psychotherapy groups. In the group, Adam felt able to open up to others for the first time, helping him to process his experience. The group consisted of people who all had some form of gender dysphoria, and included those wanting to have surgery, those who did not, those who had also regretted surgery, those with autogynaephilia, and those who were not sure as to whether they were transvestites or transgender. The group was an absolute lifeline for Adam during his otherwise suicidal depression. Adam actively engaged in the group in a way which was useful to himself and the other group members. Over a period of some years Adam was gradually able to rebuild his sense of self-esteem and his identity. His mood improved greatly as a result.

Those who had undergone sex-reassignment and still experienced gender identity problems may or may not have chosen to continue living in the cross-sex gender role. Some biological males had reverted to living in the male gender role, albeit with unwanted neo-vaginas in place of their previous male genitalia. Others had chosen to continue to live in their transgender role, albeit feeling that this was not the authentic gender solution for their problems. Some of those in the latter category described how, when they were outside of the safety of their specialist weekly psychotherapy session, they felt unable to their regrets regarding their gender reassignment, even to other health professionals. They described how they had spent years persuading professionals to allow them to access gender-reassignment, and as such, informing these same professionals of their persisting identity discomfort would have felt tantamount to an admission of failure, or even ingratitude. Some described a fear of admitting their continued identity problems to the transgender community, post-transition. They feared their admission would not be in keeping with what was expected of them and, as a result, may not be considered to be 'real transgender,' or else that people would feel 'let down' by them, leaving them ostracised by the trans community. Over the time I was running the gender dysphoria psychotherapy service, something became increasingly evident: while there was a growing awareness and acceptance of gender dysphoria amongst the general public, there was, in parallel, an increasing difficulty for a proportion of them to admit that they had changed their sex but then changed their minds. This category of transgender persons was becoming the new silent and marginalised population with no voice or representation.

Vignette: Maude

Maude had worked as a teacher. She had transitioned at the age of 40, having lived previously as a heterosexual male, albeit with a relatively asexual life and little desire for sexual relations. As a man, Maude had always had a very slight, thin build, and did not much enjoy the company of 'the rowdy men' around her. She spent many years feeling 'inauthentic' as a male, and did not identify with the versions of masculinity which she saw around her. Due to her questioning of her authenticity in her biological male role, Maude began to question whether she may be transgender in her late 30s. A little later, Maude discovered the trans club scene and managed to make some much-needed friends there who were very warm and welcoming to her. Maude's thoughts as to whether she may be transgender was confirmed to her by her transgender friends who guided her through the steps needed to pursue gender reassignment.

After a number of visits to her doctor, she persuaded him to refer her to the gender identity clinic. Maude had been briefed by her friends, and had read about what the psychiatrist at the gender identity clinic would need to be told for her to progress along the virtual conveyor belt towards being prescribed hormones and then surgery.

Maude kept all her appointments and 'said all the right things' when she was asked questions about her sense of gender identity, e.g. how certain she was in her gender identity, and how long she had felt that way. She then lived in the female gender role for a period of time prior to being prescribed hormones, and eventually, surgery.

Maude experienced a period of what I have sometimes referred to as 'gender euphoria' after her operation and felt like she was now 'one of the girls'. However, the initial feelings of excitement gradually wore off, and some years later Maude began to question whether gender reassignment had been a good idea for her. Ten years after her gender reassignment surgery, Maude referred herself to see me for an initial assessment. She told me how she had increasingly felt that her decision to have gender reassignment had been a mistake. She said that whilst she had previously felt inauthentic as a biological male, she now felt inauthentic being a trans woman, which she felt was essentially different to a biological woman. She continued to live in the female role and most people in the town she had moved to were unaware that she had previously lived as a man, or that she was trans … But Maude knew, and this, combined with her perceived sense of fraudulent inauthenticity made her feel occasionally anxious and unhappy. She had contacted me directly as she felt unable to admit to her GP that she regretted the decision to transition. Maude told me how she had spent so many years persuading health professionals to give her want she 'wanted' that now she felt too ashamed and embarrassed to admit to the doctors at the local surgery or the Gender Identity Clinic that she now felt that what she 'had previously wanted' was not actually what she 'needed'. Her post-operative 'regret' was something she would keep secret, and as such, she joined the silent proportion of those who transition and later have a change of heart. These numbers are never counted or added to a follow-up tally due to their choice to remain in silence.

Maude saw me for individual psychotherapy for a few sessions prior to being integrated into one of my weekly gender dysphoria psychotherapy groups. She became an active member and stayed in the group for a number of years. The group helped to address the post-operative 'second wave' of gender dysphoria for Maude and address her ongoing sense of gender-inauthenticity.

Most people are not aware of the differing presentations with gender dysphoria, the differences and relationship with transvestism and autogynaephilia, and the differing treatment interventions available. This includes most health professionals, including GPs, psychologists and psychiatrists working outside the field. This is a reflection of the how gender identity conditions hardly receive a mention within the training of health professionals.

So what can we do for people who have changed their sex and then changed their mind? Some of my psychotherapist colleagues had initially said that 'nothing could be done' for people who had 'wilfully chosen to castrate themselves'. Such a rigid response is dismissive, uncompassionate and punitive. It reflects some rigidity on the part of my therapist colleagues and their struggle to be able to get to grips with complex gender identity presentations. Initially it was presumed that the main therapeutic task was to 'assist in the mourning process' in relation to their previously gendered bodies. As such, the patients were placed in a group consisting solely of post-operative transsexuals who had regretted surgery. Unsurprisingly, the resulting dynamic of this group was that of being stuck in a depressing, helpless, and hopeless position without any prospect of escape. The themes of death and despair were very present, exemplified by one patient who described the recurrent dream of being chased by males and finding dead male bodies under her floorboards. When I set up my specialist service, I introduced mixed groups containing people with differing forms of gender identity conditions, including those who were post-operative. The group members were able to identify similarities and differences between each other and the resulting dynamic was far less stuck and far more hopeful. Through therapy, the members were able to explore and tailor a gender identity unique to them, irrespective of whatever hormonal or surgical interventions they were having or had had in the past. The significance of having a particular body or set of genitalia relative to their sense of gender identity was explored. Outside the field of gender dysphoria, no-one would question the validity of someone's male or female gender in the event of that person undergoing a hysterectomy or removal of other parts of their reproductive system for medical reasons such as a tumour or trauma. So in a similar vein, we encouraged the post-operative transgender group member not to feel confined to a position of *'gender-hopelessness'* simply because of any previous surgeries they may have had which they later regretted.

In some instances, there are surgical options available to those who have regretted their sex-reassignment. These operations cannot restore the original genitalia, and, as such, should not be considered as sex-reassignment reversals. This should be made clear to the potential surgical patient at the outset so that we don't build up any unrealistic expectations. The creation of a neo-phallus from a tube of tissue harvested from a forearm or their back in place of the unwanted neo-vagina may help if a person is choosing to revert to the male gender identity, provided they understand it will never feel or function in the same way as their original penis did. Nevertheless, this may be preferable to having a set of female-looking genitalia in someone now identifying as male once again.

SECTION 4

MEASURING GENDER DYSPHORIA AND TREATMENT OUTCOMES

CHAPTER 20

THE GENDER PREOCCUPATION AND STABILITY QUESTIONNAIRE (GPSQ)

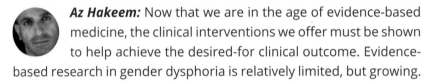 ***Az Hakeem:*** Now that we are in the age of evidence-based medicine, the clinical interventions we offer must be shown to help achieve the desired-for clinical outcome. Evidence-based research in gender dysphoria is relatively limited, but growing.

Clinicians and researchers use standardised measuring tools and outcome measures, often in the form of set questionnaires, self-report scales or interview schedules. These have all been tested and proven to be valid and reliable across differing settings and populations. There are many well-known scales for measuring depression, anxiety and other presenting conditions, which are not only useful in measuring the severity of the condition but the response to treatments, such as antidepressant medication or psychotherapy. Typically, the measuring tool will be performed during an interview with the patient, providing a score which can be compared with scores at future interviews to help ascertain symptom-change, as well as the progress and effectiveness of treatment.

When I was running my specialist gender dysphoria psychotherapy service I wanted to be able to measure its clinical effectiveness at producing the desired outcome: for the therapeutic intervention to help people be less troubled by the concept of gender in their everyday lives. I wanted them to have a stable sense of their own gender identity, irrespective of what that gender was, and irrespective of whether that stable sense of gender corresponded to their biological sex at birth, and irrespective of whether it fitted within a binary gender repertoire.

I set out looking for a suitable scale to enable me to measure the above, but unfortunately, there was no such tool in existence.

The only existing scales for use in gender identity appeared to be out-dated and heavily embedded in archaic gender stereotypes, which no longer bore much resemblance to the society in which we live. The existing scales focussed on the gender-binary, without any accommodation for those who may adopt a non-binary gender-identity such as gender-neutral, gender-queer or 'trans' (without a gendered suffix) or intersex.

There was clearly a need for such an updated measuring tool for use in gender dysphoria. With the help of my wonderful research team at the University of New South Wales, we set about devising one. The remit was to create a measuring tool, which would be of use in gender dysphoria, not only to measure the presence and / or degree of gender dysphoria, but also to help clinicians offering clinical intervention for people presenting with gender dysphoria. I did not want to limit the measuring tool for use in therapeutic interventions, but wanted it to be useful for clinicians offering medical interventions, such as hormones, for surgeons offering surgical reassignment, for therapists, counsellors, life-coaches, self-help groups, and anyone working in the field of gender dysphoria.

We wanted the tool to be quick and easy, and freely available to use without training (unlike some evaluation tools, which are copyrighted, require the user to embark on training, and pay for the privilege). We wanted to devise a tool, which was useful and universally available for widespread use, not something from which we could generate money.

Interventions for people with gender dysphoria have the common goal of assisting people to achieve stability in their gender identity (rather than their sense of gender changing from day to day). We want to help them be happy in their gender so that they are less troubled and less preoccupied by gender on a day-to-day basis. That, after all, is the aim of the hormone-prescribing physicians, the surgeons who carry out the gender-reassignment surgery, and those of us who concentrate on therapeutic interventions. With this in mind, we named the measuring tool the Gender Preoccupation and Stability Questionnaire (GPSQ).

Aims of the GPSQ:

- Detect and measure gender dysphoria
- Measure degree of preoccupation with gender
- Measure extent of the stability of gender-identity
- Not limit repertoire of genders to binary
  (male / female) framework
- Acknowledge that gender does not have to correspond to
  biological sex at birth
- Accommodate non-binary, gender-neutral / gender-queer and
  intersex gender-identities
- Be easy to use
- Ensure it is not time-consuming to administer
- Be widely available and free to use

A questionnaire was devised which comprises some initial brief demographic questions followed by 14 questions. The GPSQ questionnaire was then tested for its validity and reliability by our research team in a pilot study. The aims of the pilot study were to check to see if it worked in detecting gender dysphoria, and to ensure the GPSQ did not produce any operating errors (known as 'false positives' or 'false negatives') when used in populations who may have co-existing mental health problems.

The GPSQ was used alongside an existing valid and reliable tool, the Gender Identity / Gender Dysphoria Questionnaire for Adolescents and Adults (GIDYQ-AA). The existing measure against which we were comparing the GPSQ was well established but had separate scales for 'males' and 'females' and did not accommodate non-binary, gender-queer or intersex gender identities.

The pilot study would not have been possible without the help of my friends and colleagues in the Australia and New Zealand Professional Association for Transgender Health (ANZPATH). Professional colleagues in ANZPATH distributed the GPSQ and the existing tool to people with gender identity conditions under their care who had consented to participate. This part of the study enabled the research team to ascertain how the GPSQ compared to the existing tool in being able to detect gender dysphoria.

The second part of the study was to use the GPSQ on a population of people who reported not having a gender dysphoria (asked as a screening question on this part of the study) but who did have a serious mental health condition. We wanted to see if the presence of a serious mental health condition would render the GPSQ invalid by producing aberrant results. For this population, we used consenting mental health patients at the hospital, where the research team and myself were based.

The third arm of the study was to test the GPSQ on a population of people who had neither a gender dysphoria, nor serious mental health condition (both excluded via initial screening questions) and for this population, we used consenting members of staff working across all clinical and non-clinical roles within the hospital where we were based.

We used a rigorous statistical analysis of the findings once the study was complete. The GPSQ was shown to be a valid tool for identifying gender dysphoria with scores of 28 or more indicating the presence of gender dysphoria. The GPSQ was also shown to be a valid tool for measuring the degree of gender preoccupation and measuring the stability of one's gender identity. The presence of any co-existing mental illnesses does not appear to be a problem for the use of the tool as there were no erroneous results when used in the pilot group with mental illness.

The GPSQ is unique in that it is the only valid and reliable tool for measuring gender dysphoria:

- It can measure the effectiveness of most interventions aimed at those with a gender dysphoria.
- It does not necessitate gender roles as corresponding to biological sex at birth.
- It not limited to an out-dated repertoire of binary (male / female) gender roles.
- It is able to accommodate non-binary gender identities including gender-neutral, gender-queer, 'trans' and intersex.

A copy of the GPSQ questionnaire is included in the appendix at the end of this book. Please feel free to use and distribute it, and incorporate it into any future research and evaluation of gender-identity interventions and services.

To apply for a gender recognition certificate:

- Applicants have to be at least 18 years of age
- Must be living in the 'other gender', or …
- Must have changed gender under the law of a country outside the UK
- Must apply to a Gender Recognition Panel

The Gender Recognition Panel is able to grant the certificate if:

- The applicant has had gender dysphoria as confirmed either by two doctors, or one doctor and a psychologist, at least one of which should be a specialist in the field of gender dysphoria
- The applicant has lived in the acquired gender role for at least two years
- They intend to continue living in the acquired gender role until their death

SECTION 5

TRANSGENDER POLITICS

CHAPTER 21

THE GENDER RECOGNITION ACT (UK)

Az Hakeem: The Gender Recognition Act is a piece of legislation in the UK, which was passed on July 1st 2004. The act makes provision for changing one's gender status and the issuing of a 'gender recognition certificate'. The Act enables people to apply to have the legal status of their gender changed and receive a gender recognition certificate, as long as a number of conditions are fulfilled.

Where a full gender recognition certificate is issued, a person is able to legally adopt the acquired gender status. This entitles them to the legal rights of persons in the acquired gender status. This had previously given the right to marry someone of the opposite sex to their acquired gender, or enter into a civil partnership with a person of the same biological sex as their acquired gender, and new legislation in the UK now permits members of the same sex to enter into marriage. The person with a gender recognition certificate will be able to have the same pension and benefits rights of persons in their acquired gender, and change legal documentation such as their passport. The Gender Recognition Act makes a point of stating that it does not affect things done, or events occurring, before the certificate is issued. However, it does enable a birth certificate to be issued in the new acquired gender. This has caused some controversy as many people are of the opinion that a birth certificate is a historical document recording the details of an event in time. Consequently it may not be reversed or changed after that date, irrespective of what changes the person makes subsequently in their lives, or how much we may wish an event had never happened, or that it had happened differently.

Changing one's gender and being issued with a Gender Recognition Certificate does not change the outcome of inheritance and does not influence the descent of any peerage, dignity or title of honour. Similarly, a full gender recognition certificate does not enable the person to evade criminal responsibility for any gender-specific crimes being attempted or committed. The Gender Recognition Act does not require competitive sporting events to recognise the acquired gender status as this may confer unfair advantage.

Whilst the Gender Recognition Act safeguards the privacy of those to whom a Gender Recognition Certificate is issued, the act does allow this 'protected information' to be disclosed if there are valid public policy reasons such as may occur in the investigation or prevention of a crime, or in accordance with an order of a court or tribunal.

CHAPTER 22

TRANSGENDER POLITICS

Melissa Vick: Trans politics is complicated. Political work, whether by trans people with others or, occasionally, 'for' us, takes a number of forms, expresses a wide range of different views, and is directed at many different issues, ideas, institutions, and groups. Our political engagements may seem energetic, fractious and combative, but they are shaped by our experience.

For the non-trans people who work with us and share our lives, it is useful to understand our concerns and the politics through which we address them. It is also important to appreciate, as far as is possible, that what drives our politics is our experience of living in an often-hostile world. This short chapter cannot hope to do justice to everything, so I will focus mainly on trans women's politics, since I know them from the inside out.

LOBBYING AND INSTITUTIONAL ENGAGEMENT

Trans people find their means of political action in different ways. Some are similar to mainstream lobby group politics; Australia's *A Gender Agenda* [AGA] is a good example. One aspect of its work is lobbying politicians, government departments, and local businesses and organisations, advocating on behalf of the trans community. It works with those individuals and organisations to help them understand priorities for changes in legislation and administration. It helps them frame strategies and policies for improving conditions for all of us, and it trains and educates staff to work more appropriately with trans people. To support this work, it engages with researchers to shape their agendas, and provides useable information about trans needs. In the United States, much of this work is done through the more broadly focused American Civil Liberties Union [ACLU] and focused on legal action defending trans rights and trans supportive legislation, often case by case, opposing discriminatory legislation and appealing discriminatory court rulings.

A relatively new form of political action is more highly individualised, and involves online 'grass roots' petitioning through organisations such as *Change.org*. A good example is the petition initiated by Australian teenager Georgie Stone, to repeal the legislation that requires Family Court approval to undertake hormone therapy prior to the age of legal majority. Supported by intensive lobbying from Georgie and her supporters, this aims to remove what had been a prohibitively expensive barrier for many trans teens.

Such lobbying and related activity, then, is either collective or individual, focused on single issues or more general trans rights and needs, and in the cases of collective action, is generated from either dedicated trans organisations or bodies with a broader progressive agenda.

DEVELOPING IDEAS AND KNOWLEDGE

Much trans politics involves developing ideas and knowledge about trans people, about the conditions that shape our lives, and about how to understand and improve them.

A lot of it takes place online and there is an extensive resource of blogs. The views expressed vary widely, in ways that reflect the variety of our concerns, and the many different ways we have of understanding and living our lives as trans people. Sometimes these views are strongly argued from research; sometimes they express individual experiences, values, and goals.

Unlike lobby group politics, this form of political activity is not necessarily directed towards specific institutions or groups, and does not necessarily aim to achieve specific outcomes. However, it has an important role in fostering argument and debate. The understanding it helps to develop is taken up as part of trans community knowledge for understanding and engaging with the world we live in. A good example of this is the development of the concept of 'cisnormativity,' which I discuss below. It was initially developed in trans blogs, where it became a key term for many trans social, cultural and political analyses. From there, it has made its way into the academic literature, where it challenges the professional understandings that impact on our lives.

Research, when conducted by trans people, or in close consultation with us, is highly important as a form of political activity. Of the growing volume of such trans-led and trans-friendly research, a tiny handful of examples serve to illustrate the nature of this work. The social-psychological work of Kristina Olsen and colleagues at University of Washington carefully and critically dissects much of the earlier literature about young trans people and 'desistance' – appearing to be trans in childhood and returning to being cisgender in adolescence. This has shown that the apparent high rates of 'desistance' are largely a product of lack of precision in the research. Their original research documents the mental health of prepubescent children who have socially transitioned (i.e., are living in the gender with which they identify, 'opposite' from that which they were assigned at birth) with appropriate support. The work of social researchers such as Greta Bauer and colleagues, Jake Pyne, and Dean Spade, document a range of social and legal practices and conditions that shape the quality of our lives – and in many, many cases, put them at risk. And scholars such as Raewyn Connell explore conceptual issues, such as the nature of gender, and the strategic concerns, such as the relationship between trans people and feminism.

This work is complemented by research-informed writing by authors such as Vivienne Namaste and Julia Serano, which draw on, rather than actively generate, research to address a wide range of conceptual and social issues facing trans people and affecting our wellbeing.

While such work has much less immediate public visibility and impact than many other forms of political action, it has the potential to improve the knowledge base from which medical, administrative and legal regimes directly affect trans people's lives. Perhaps even more importantly, it has the potential to challenge the norms and assumptions within which such knowledge is generated and framed.

BUILDING COMMUNITY

A third form of trans political work involves building community. This takes place in both 'traditional' local and regional organisations, and online. Online community-building sites include dedicated trans sites (e.g. *Wipe Out Transphobia, Pink Essence*), and trans groups within both open 'mainstream' sites such as Facebook and 'closed' networking sites such as *FetLife* (which hosts groups such as '20s something and trans,' '*Rethinking Trans*' and '*An Impenetrable Queer And Trans Fortress On FetLife*').

Such groups are diverse in membership and focus. Facebook, for example, includes:

- Open (often mixed trans and non-trans memberships) groups, such as 'Support for education on gender issues'
- Closed (searchable but with restricted membership) groups
- Secret (not searchable and with membership by invitation) groups

Fetlife provides a community online (but designed to facilitate local connections) for those of us whose understanding of ourselves is enmeshed with our histories of seeking to resolve the tensions, self-hatred, and the desires we experience, through masochism, cross dressing, and forced feminisation, within relationships built around explicit domination and submission. For many of us, this community remains important after transition as a means of finding sexual partners who will accept us in the face of the rejection we often encounter from others.

A profusion of local organisations work to build community through formal and informal 'real life' support groups and networks which meet more or less regularly. The political potential of such groups is again well illustrated by *A Gender Agenda*. Alongside its lobbying roles, it organises or provides counselling, a social 'drop in' morning, a fitness group and other services, actively building the social and personal strengths and support networks of its members, and linking the trans community with the 'community at large'. Its capacity to do so is enhanced by its formal organisation, the breadth of its activities and its level of ambition. Together, these have given it a vision and a capacity to secure funding for at least some of its activities and thus further build its organisational strength. In my own local community, there is a long standing but largely defunct organisation of mainly older trans women, an active group of younger trans adults and children, and parents of those children. More informally, the local gender clinic has often connected me, as a senior trans person in the community to others beginning transition, or isolated in their transition. Even more informally, I've often used my dinner table as a place to bring trans people together to get to know each other and build a sense of solidarity amongst us.

Many such groups and informal networks have limited reach into their local trans communities because of factors including age and personality, as well as differences in our needs, and our ways of living as trans people. However, they may also be connected to wider online networks. Such groups and networks, whether local or online, offer a sense of solidarity, and help share ideas for understanding and engaging an often hostile 'outside' world.

MEDIA AND RESEARCH

Some trans politics involves contributing to highly specialist and privileged activities, e.g. film-making, production of TV news and documentaries, speaking to mass media etc. Here, both trans people and our allies are important, although many trans people stress how it is crucial that we have direct input into, if not leadership of such work, so that it reflects our experience and understandings, not just someone else's idea of our experience and needs.

Examples of such 'trans-friendly' media activity include:

- Films and television programmes such as *52 Tuesdays*, *Boy meets Girl*, *3 Generations*, *Transparent*, the mini-series *Her Story*, and teenager Jazz Jennings's show, *I am Jazz*, on *The Learning Channel* are specifically about transition and trans lives. Others, such as *Orange is the New Black*, feature, but do not focus on, trans characters, realistically and / or sympathetically, in contrast to the historical tendency to include trans characters as caricatures and / or figures of derision, contempt or fear.

- News or documentary programmes that feature and explore trans people's experiences and lives. These include, for instance, the UK's Nine Lives Media's *Sam and Evan: from girls to men*x trans men and their growing relationship, highlighting different family reactions, and the trans and homophobic hostility they encountered in their local community. In Australia, the ABC's *Four Corners* programme *Being Me*, which focused especially on the social transition of a primary (elementary) school girl, and two Australian Story episodes which featured, respectively, the transitions of Catherine Macgregor, a high ranking military officer, and a teenaged trans girl, Georgie Stone and her family, in an episode dealing, in particular, with the legal requirement to secure Family Court approval for medically supported transition.

• Newspaper and magazine reports, feature articles and opinion pieces, starting, perhaps, with the *Boston Globe's* careful and richly detailed account of Nicole Maines' transition, with attention given to the family, school and medical aspects of the process. More recently there has been coverage in major newspapers like the *NY Times, The Guardian, Washington Post,* and the *LA Times*, and magazines such as *Time, New Scientist,* and *National Geographic*, as well as more regional newspapers.

• Trans input into mass media includes public appearances and contributions to the discussion of trans issues by a range of high profile figures. Some, like Caitlyn Jenner, are considered relatively controversial in trans circles. But notable significant appearances include the interview of trans model Carmen Carrera and actress Laverne Cox, by TV host Katie Couric. While the show was ostensibly about their careers, Couric quickly shifted topic to ask about the women's genitalia. While Carrera deflected this as 'inappropriately personal,' Cox responded by bluntly pointing out the inappropriateness of any such questions. Asking them, she explained, was not only prurient and objectifying, but also deflected attention from matters such as poverty, discrimination, and violence that confront many trans women and threaten their wellbeing and, often, their lives.

What makes such varied media treatment, in which trans people's contributions are crucial, so politically important is that it educates and challenges misunderstanding and prejudice across very large audiences. Increasingly, in my judgement, such media representation of trans people and our issues has become more sympathetic. It is beginning to represent us in a positive and supportive manner, and challenging the hostile representations of us that were once commonplace (and continue to be perpetuated in many openly conservative media outlets).

AIMS AND TARGETS

Trans politics reflects a variety of aims and is directed at a range of targets, including broad cultural conditions, legal, social, political systems, and particular social groupings whom many of us perceive as hostile to us in various ways.

Legal protections

One important aim is to secure the extension of various legal protections and rights to include us, such as anti-discrimination legislation, policy and procedures. This is important where, for example, it is still legal to dismiss employees on the grounds that they are trans, as is the case in many US states.

A related aim is to secure change to the administrative practices that make our lives needlessly more difficult than they are for non-trans people. It is often difficult for us to secure identity documents, which match our lived identities and presentations as men or women, in everyday life. This inspires advocacy and action designed to address the barriers we face securing legal ratification of our lived sex / gender, and identity documents that allow us to deal with the large number of social situations in which these documents are required (from enrolling in school or college, or applying for jobs, through opening bank accounts, to dealing with social security agencies), without 'outing' ourselves and putting us unnecessarily at risk.

One very specific political issue to do with public life and gender identity that attracts considerable attention from trans and non-trans people alike is the right to use public lavatories (toilets, bathrooms, public accommodations, etc.) that match our identity and self-presentation rather than the gender we were assigned at birth. This is important because we are at risk if we use lavatories designed for our 'legal' sex - the sex we were assigned at birth – because of the difference between our appearance and the sex of the facility. However, in many places, if we use the facility that matches our gender identity and appearance, we are also at risk, both legally and physically, in the face of potential violence from others.

The 'bathroom' issue in the US provides a good illustration of some of the complexities in trans politics. The success of the 'gay marriage' movement in some respects opened the way for trans issues to become 'the next civil rights frontier'. And, indeed, there were a number of successful moves to introduce legal protections for trans people. However, our increased visibility, and the introduction of tangible legal protections, also provided both a trigger and a focus for a conservative backlash – which has gained enormous social, political and legal impetus with the election of Donald Trump as President.

'Backlash' bathroom laws require people to use (public) bathrooms corresponding to the gender attributed to them at birth. These have been vigorously contested by bodies such as the ACLU, and opposed or resisted by a range of businesses, major sporting bodies and other 'progressive' organisations. Trans people, too, have counter-attacked using, among other approaches, the circulation of posters showing very macho (trans) men and very sexualised and stereotypically feminine (trans) women in the bathrooms of their original legal genders, with captions such as: 'Do you really want someone like me in your [husband's / wife's / daughter's] bathroom'?

The attacks on trans people's bathroom use have attributed criminality and deception to trans women, and deployed highly conservative, antifeminist rhetoric encouraging men to protect their wives and daughters. Often, they have openly or implicitly incited violence against trans people. Practically, too, such moves have resulted in attacks not only on trans women (already widely subject to such violence) but on 'butch'-presenting cisgender women, drawing on, and in turn, reinforcing, conservative norms of gender presentation. Trans people, too, have pointed out that the 'Do you want me in their bathrooms' campaigns also reinforced such norms – which put many 'non-passing' and queer-presenting trans people at risk - by presenting only very 'passing' trans men and women.

Whatever the complexities of these campaigns, they all aim to secure legal protections for trans people, against the discriminations that put our economic welfare, social and cultural legitimacy, and physical safety and emotional wellbeing at risk.

Multiple disadvantages (intersectionality)

A quite different aim for some trans politics is to secure change to legal conditions and social practices that make a significant sector of the trans population highly vulnerable. Often such vulnerability reflects multiple disadvantages – colour, education, employment, health (including mental health), and criminal record. Such factors not only co-exist but interact, compounding each other in ways that are well-articulated in Kimberly Crenshaw's concept of 'intersectionality', to create significant problems for ensuring survival, let alone wellbeing.

Thus, for example, women of colour grow up facing personal discrimination based on race and gender, and systemic structural inequality. Systemic structural inequality makes it likely that their families will be relatively poor, that they will access underfunded and over stressed schools offering limited opportunities for educational success and in turn yielding access to secure, well paid, let alone rewarding employment. Being trans they are likely to face further discrimination, violence, and homelessness if they seek to transition and emotional stress, and potential mental illness if they don't. Whether transitioning or not, they will struggle to access appropriate health care. Regardless of educational qualifications, if they are identified as trans, they will be subject to further discrimination in employment. Such complex, compounding disadvantages lead many trans women into sex work; this puts them further at risk of violence on the streets, of recurrent arrest and a growing criminal record. This will react back on any attempts they may make at seeking other employment, and often lead to further violence when they are incarcerated, as is common, in male prisons, despite either their gender presentation or even their documented legal status as women.

While middle class, white trans women also face a range of discriminations and other risks, this example demonstrates how more disadvantaged backgrounds generate compounding problems.

A key challenge for trans politics is to ensure that those of us who enjoy relatively privileged backgrounds speak and organise not just for ourselves but for those facing such multiple oppressions.

The medical profession

The medical profession is of special interest to much of trans politics. Partly, this is because, for most of us, access to hormones, the monitoring of associated health risks, and to a lesser extent surgery, are crucial to our transition and our sense of wellbeing. A major concern is access to quality medical support and care. There is a widespread sense among us, well supported by research, that many practitioners do not understand trans issues and needs, do not listen to us, do not accept our own understandings of ourselves, and continue to address us using names and pronouns we do not accept for ourselves. Critiques of the medical profession at this level are often quite specific and may be directed personally at individual practitioners. They often express a general sense of (mutual) mistrust, even hostility, where trust is of the essence, and may feed into broader forms of political critique and action.

Such broader critiques focus on systemic issues around the medical profession and the health care systems in which it is embedded. Concerns range from the costs of access to health services, through the shortage of trans-specialist healthcare services, to the lack of relevant training and knowledge of practitioners. Relatively tangible forms of political action to address at least some of these concerns include lobbying for more, and more accessible, specialist services, and for the incorporation of more, and more accurate, knowledge about trans health in the education of both prospective and practising health professionals. Trans political work in this domain seeks to build more productive relationships between trans people and the health professions through consultation and working groups, joint conferences and workshops.

A more fundamental concern is the power and authority of the medical profession to determine the shape of our lives, and the body of psychiatric knowledge, which the exercise of this power draws on. Access to the medical support for transition that is considered standard for trans people, certainly in the relatively affluent west, is dependent on convincing a doctor or a psychiatrist, or both, that we meet their criteria. These criteria are laid out in *DSM (the Diagnostic and Statistical Manual of Mental Disorders*, currently version 5). Some trans people argue that being included in DSM already pathologises us, in that it puts us under the banner of suffering from a mental illness, even if the term gender dysphoria no longer classifies us, as DSM did in past versions, as having a 'disorder'. Others, however, argue that our incorporation in a list of medical conditions is necessary for us to access the trans-specific medical support that we seek for our transitions.

Much of the psychiatric research which informs the *DSM* criteria is concerned with identifying the characteristics of 'real' trans people. It has provided the basis for the singular, narrow view that 'real' trans people experience themselves as being of 'the opposite' gender to the one that is assumed to correspond to their genitalia - that they feel 'trapped in the wrong body'. However, many of us who live as trans men and women, do not experience ourselves that way. It is widely understood among trans communities that unless we present such a narrative of our lives to our assessing psychiatrists, we will be deemed (as many of us have been) to be 'merely fetishists' rather than 'genuinely' trans. This understanding fuels the pressure for us to present that narrative, even if it is not true to our experience; this, in turn, feeds the view, clearly expressed in some of the psychiatric and other literature, that we are not to be trusted.

A fundamental concern of much trans politics, then, is the assumption that we are best understood in medical terms, and supported by laws and codes of medical practice; in other words, that doctors and psychiatrists are better placed to judge whether we are 'really' trans than we are ourselves. This in turn gives the medical practitioners we approach for support and assistance the power to provide or withhold that support, and to effectively enable or block our transitions. Thus, a significant target for trans politics is what is widely seen, and attacked, as the 'gatekeeping' role of medical practitioners, judging the authenticity and validity of our experiential self-knowledge, keeping out 'pretenders' rather than facilitating access to medical support by those who encounter us as trans. In its place, many of us advocate a model of 'informed consent' where health practitioners provide advice and information about various options for dealing with our sense of being trans but leave the decisions about whether and how to proceed to us.

Much more specific medical targets have been high profile medical figures who are widely seen by trans activists as hostile and transphobic, using their positions in prestigious institutions to legitimise views that work against our recognition and supportive treatment. The removal (or at least the partial discrediting) of such figures can be seen, in part, as successful outcomes of this form of trans political action.

Prejudice

A quite different, more diffuse and broad ranging trans politics targets prejudice. The word transphobia is used colloquially, just as homophobia is used, to describe a generalised negativity in attitude or behaviour towards trans people on the basis of our trans-ness. Political activity around transphobia takes the form of education through dissemination of information at a variety of levels, from personal explanation, through print and online materials, to participation in seminars and workshops. Often, this is opportunistic, a response to transphobic incidents or comments, such as Laverne Cox's response to Katie Couric, mentioned earlier. Indeed, this educational activity complements the contribution to developing a more trans-friendly media, and the organisational engagement in training I mentioned earlier.

Cultural beliefs about gender: cisnormativity and erasure

At the broadest and most encompassing level, trans cultural politics targets cisnormativity, by critiquing the complex ways it shapes social, political and institutional aspects of prejudice and oppression (including the role of the medical profession in 'managing' us, and the ways psychiatry often understands us). Cisnormativity is a set of ideas, and the practices which reflect them, that assume 'sex' is binary (male or female), that 'gender' is necessarily and always the same as 'sex', and that people live in the gender they were assigned at birth. Moreover, it assumes that genders, bodies, and personal identities match each other. Overall, social life, from top to bottom, reflects these assumptions. It takes cisgender people as the embodiment of gender norms, and judges trans people by their non / conformity to those norms.

This concept provides a way to analyse the cultural views and practices which frame how gender works to shape people's understandings of gender and gender issues, including trans issues. In particular, it provides a way of understanding what many of us call 'erasure': how the very existence of trans people is so widely seen as impossible, e.g. 'You've got a penis, you can't be a woman'! Indeed, our knowledge of ourselves as trans is commonly seen as a delusion, and disregarded. It also helps explain why, since we challenge such deeply rooted norms about gender – norms that are fundamental to non-trans people's own identities as men and women – we are so readily excluded from 'normal' human rights. Moreover, it illustrates why the issue of access to appropriate lavatories is so inflammatory, and why we are so frequently targets of violence.

An extension of this form of political critique is the work of making us both visible, and understandable as normal, ordinary human beings. This asserts our legitimacy, encourages recognition of the broad diversity of ways in which people experience their gender and thus works to weaken prejudice at an individual level. It gives an understanding of gender that supports change in the way gender is managed in legislation, regulation, policy and practice. While political targets are admittedly amorphous, those who engage in such political activity point out that such rethinking of gender is fundamental to the social and cultural changes which are necessary, in the long term, to enable us to live our lives with a sense of security.

An important strand of such educative politics aims to make others aware of the multiple ways in which many trans people are disadvantaged. Multiple disadvantages include the compounding of the effects of being trans and the social structures that work against those who are disabled, a person of colour, or a non-native speaker in the country they live in. They also include what we might think of as the sequential, accumulating effects of struggling with our identity as children and young adolescents, with lack of family support, leading to depression and self-harm, disengagement from school, and ultimately, to difficulty finding employment, and poverty.

Schools

Given the increasing number of people presenting as trans, and socially transitioning in childhood, schools have become an increasingly important focus for trans politics. Anti-discrimination legislation, policy and legal judgements, newspaper articles, programme materials, children's books, and the minutiae of individual school practices have all constituted part of the struggle over trans rights in education.

In the US, trans activists, working with the ACLU (as noted earlier) have lobbied against State-wide legislation, and fought multiple individual case battles to secure or protect trans students' access to the school bathrooms, and to a lesser extent changing rooms, that match the gender in which they live their lives. Such struggles have occupied the same general ideological terrain as noted earlier regarding 'bathroom' politics more broadly. Trans advocates and the parents of the trans students concerned have in many cases been highly active in advocating to school boards, speaking in public forums and to local media, as well as writing to and in local newspapers, explaining their situations and educating school officials and politicians, and the public at large on the basic issues of human rights and human dignity such matters involve.

In Australia, the strong Christian and other right-wing lobbies associated with the conservative coalition Commonwealth government have mounted strong opposition to a range of progressive social policies, and have found a target to attack in the Safe Schools programme. Safe Schools, which enjoyed a period of Commonwealth government funding, offers a suite of educative and resource materials that aim to support gay and gender 'nonconforming' students in their own processes of self-discovery, self-acceptance, and self-affirmation, and to educate teachers and students about gender and sexuality to build the understandings from which a more accepting, inclusive school environment can grow. They also provide support for school leaders and administrators seeking more inclusive and supportive policies and school-wide practices. The defence of the Safe Schools programme has, consequently, been a significant focus for a wide range of progressive bodies, including trans activists.

But such visible battles are paralleled by less visible, local political action to ensure that individual schools provide both a progressive gender and sexuality curriculum and a safe and supportive environment for all – including trans – students. Such local actions are not isolated from the broader struggles. This is nicely illustrated in an exemplary case in my own local community. A progressive policy environment, such as that provided by this and some other State governments, and supported by the Safe Schools organisation and its resources, have come together to provide a positive context for local schools to facilitate their students' transitions. This context, together with a more accepting cultural context, and the community-building work of the local gender clinic had connected me with the family of a 9-year-old girl beginning transition. At that stage, selected teachers, counsellors, senior staff, the girl herself (who was still not presenting at school as a girl), and her parents, met recurrently to discuss, plan, support and monitor her transition. In my judgement, the supportive tone of that process was illustrated by the Principal's comment to the 9-year-old in one such meeting: 'This is your transition; we need you to tell us when you are ready for... or uncomfortable with ...'

'Enemies'

Finally, there are a number of specific groupings and activities that are the focus of trans politics. Perhaps what attracts the most intense ire of many trans activists are the self-described 'radfems', and events, such as radfem conferences, and the Michigan Womyn's (sic) Music Festival, that explicitly exclude trans women. They attack and exclude us on the grounds that we are not really women at all. Radfem ideas and explicitly trans-exclusive women's events are relatively marginal minority ideologies and activities, and have less impact on most trans people's lives than, say, difficulties in securing identity documentation, or access to quality health services. Nonetheless, because they deny our existence so vehemently, and exclude us so pointedly, they attract heated and vocal opposition among some circles of trans activities. Much of this opposition takes the form of critiquing their ideas and seeking access for trans women to events that are billed as 'for women'. More broadly, an important strand of trans women's politics aims at recognition by, and inclusion in, feminist politics more generally.

Right-wing (including many Christian) lobbies are also common targets of trans political action. Such groups commonly represent us as an impossibility, suggesting that we seek to undermine the natural order (inaccurately claiming a scientific perspective for a rigid cisnormative, binary understanding of sex and gender). Elsewhere they portray us as a social threat, undermining the sanctity and stability of the heterosexual family. And yet again, they suggest that we are deceivers and predators seeking to take advantage of access to gender appropriate bathrooms to prey on innocent women and girls (despite no evidence that such a threat actually exists). In a variation of that theme, they argue that granting our rights will provide opportunity and cover for predatory cis males (despite the fact that legal protections against such behaviour already exist). Trans campaigns contest such claims, and lobby against legislation and regulations that reflects such views.

Such conservative lobbies also strongly oppose (and, in Trump's America, seek to re-open the issue of) 'gay marriage', a matter that affects many trans people's relationships. Many trans people and groups have been active in campaigns to secure same-sex marriage, typically in conjunction with LGB allies. Such campaigns often, either explicitly or by implication, challenge conservative norms of gender and sexuality.

At times, however, trans activists find ourselves at odds with our LGB 'allies'. Often, it appears to us, we are useful collaborators in the long campaigns to achieve a range of legal rights (marriage equality is a good example, here). However, it appears that, once the dominant groups' goals are secured, or even as a trade-off for securing those goals, they distance themselves from us, seeing an alliance with us as no longer being in their best interests. In such circumstances, we have seen our own particular needs and concerns left to languish.

DIFFERENCES AMONG US

While we devote much political activity to issues arising from social structures and conditions, as well as from non-trans people, we also invest considerable energy into dealing with differences among us. These include differences of interest arising from our varied experiences as trans people, our divergent understandings of trans-ness, and the alternative priorities that these generate. They also include differences over priorities, practices and strategies.

Differences of interest: inclusions and exclusions

The differences among us in our experience of being trans and our understandings of what it is to be trans give rise to conflicting interests among us. Thus, despite the issues we face in common, trans women may face distinctive issues, understand ourselves differently, and see our needs and interests differently from trans men, or from those trans people who identify as gender-queer, or who are also intersex. There are similar sorts of differences between trans women who are 'non-op', 'pre-op' and 'post-op', and between those who are living 'in stealth' and those who are more open about their trans status and gender history. Take, for instance, 'post op' trans women who understand being trans in terms of the 'wrong body' narrative, who seek to be understood simply as 'women' (without the 'trans' prefix) and to live in stealth. They are likely to want ease of changing documents for themselves, but may not consider extending the same right to, say, trans women, who have not had any surgery. They are likely to disagree with those of us who see our best interests lie in easing the criteria for securing changes in identity documents for *any* who identify as trans, or making the diversity of trans women more visible.

There are two issues at stake here. One is what we might call the politics of embodiment: the right to claim the 'authenticity' of our own respective experiences of embodiment as trans people. Some post-op trans women consider those of us who claim to be trans, but regard surgery to convert our penises into vaginas as unnecessary or undesirable, to not be truly trans at all. In contrast, many of us experience ourselves as trans women but see no contradictions in having a penis, and also regard ourselves as 'authentically' trans and seek to have ourselves recognised just as truly trans as anyone else.

The second issue is what we might call the politics of representation: the struggle over the various ways we might be represented. Some of us have never understood ourselves as 'trapped in the wrong body', for instance, or don't experience any contradiction between identifying and living as a woman and having a penis. Some of us identify and / or present ourselves in ways that don't fit neatly into the male / female binary; we push for a highly differentiated representation of what it is to be trans, among the trans community, as well as in research and in the media. The concern for an accurate representation of what it is to be trans involves conflicts within the trans world that largely parallel differences over the politics of embodiment.

The politics of representation also involves concerns with language. On the one hand, we tend to be concerned about the language used to refer to us. We insist on the use of appropriate pronouns, such as 'she' for trans women; 'he' for trans men and 'they' for those who identify as gender queer. And some of us campaign against the use of terms such as 'shemales', and 'chicks with dicks' which many of us find offensive. Many of us also contest the use of terms like 'tranny', which confuse us with 'mere' crossdressers ('transvestites') in ways that lead to misunderstandings of what it means to be trans and many (but not all) of us argue vehemently that 'crossdressers' have not right to use the title 'trans'.

An important group of trans activists are also concerned with the even broader issue of inclusiveness in trans politics. Reflecting the way significant parts of the trans population are affected by the compound effect of multiple intersecting disadvantages, as I noted above, we argue that many of the political struggles trans people engage in are essentially concerned with trans people who are relatively privileged. We seek to promote a broader, more inclusive political agenda, and insist that priority be accorded to issues of widespread poverty and violence, including violence by police, and the interests and needs of, for example, sex workers and homeless trans folk.

Aims and strategies

A quite different division over priorities concerns the choice of broad strategic aims. On the one hand, there are those who argue that fundamental gains require fundamental social and cultural shifts, and stress the importance of the politics of representation associated with the critique of cisnormativity. On the other, there are those who focus on concrete gains in legislation, policy and administrative procedure, and on the provision of better-informed and 'friendlier' health services and less discriminatory social services more generally. To the first group, the second may appear to be engaged in a sticking plaster approach. To the second group, the first approach may well appear to commit to an important but idealistic long-term goal, but ignore the immediate and pressing needs and difficulties of trans people now.

This division is often reflected in critiques that seek the extension of legal protections to explicitly include trans people. While characteristically acknowledging the importance of such extensions, and the work of those whose efforts help secure them, the people engaged in cultural and structural critique point out the limited applicability of many protections and inclusions for trans people as a whole. They argue that the right to secure a change in a passport gender has no perceptible benefit for trans people in poverty, and protections against workplace discrimination offer nothing to the high numbers of trans people unable to secure work, or who are engaged in sex work.

Divisions of interest and priority are also reflected in differences regarding what is commonly referred to as 'umbrella politics' – the forming of broad coalitions around widely shared interests. On the one hand, many trans activists who believe that all trans people share a solid core of interests across our differences, and actually share some of these interests with others in the LBJ spectrum (e.g. freedom from discrimination in employment and marriage). Those of us who take that view seek to join forces with others on the basis of those shared interests, with a view to increasing our political impact. However, many others emphasise the distinctive interests we have as trans people rather than, or over and above, those we might share with gay or bisexual people. Those of us who stress our differences highlight the risk of diluting or sacrificing our own specific needs in broad coalitions, and point to cases where the reforms we have helped our allies to secure have failed to include us in their benefits.

TRANSGENDER POLITICS – SUMMARY

Trans politics is a diverse field marked by different approaches, different views, and different 'targets'. Crucially, our politics are grounded in our diverse experiences of marginalisation and oppression. We strive to understand ourselves and secure living conditions that support our attempts to live our lives safely, richly, and with dignity. Understanding the diversity of our politics and of our political concerns is an important step towards understanding us.

CHAPTER 23

TRANSGENDER POLITICS:
A CLINICIAN'S PERSONAL EXPERIENCE

EVERYONE TO BE TREATED EQUALLY DOES NOT MEAN EVERYONE IS PERCEIVED TO BE THE SAME

Az Hakeem: There is a small yet very vocal politically driven sub-population within transgender activists (transactivisits) whose agenda appears (either intentionally or otherwise) to be for all persons with gender dysphoria to be considered the same: as transsexuals without any differences between them or their particular gender dysphoria. They suggest that there is no person-to-person variation, assuming that as a population, they are 'homogenous' rather than 'heterogenous'. They are also keen to advocate that the only valid and useful clinical intervention is physical sex-reassignment with hormones / surgery, and for this to be universally provided to everyone with any gender dysphoria, with the minimal input from psychotherapists or psychiatrists. Some even go as far as to suggest that transgender people should not be offered any exploratory psychotherapy. Whilst they truly believe that this politically driven cause is for the good of all those with gender dysphoria, it is difficult to see how their proposal for people to be denied a variety of health interventions could be considered progress.

Unfortunately, the political trans activists who are most vocal in the press and social media are often given the status of unelected spokespersons for 'the trans community'. Although I am never quite sure which particular 'community' this refers to, and my trans patients have often similarly been confused about what this community was, and whether they were part of it. With the militant trans activist being presumed / assumed as spokesperson for 'the trans community' this only serves to hide the extent of bullying and intimidation. This may include cyber-bullying and direct personal attacks aimed at people who are felt to provide opinion that is contrary to a particularly rigid and prescribed way of thinking about gender dysphoria.

Fortunately, there is a growing body of people within the transgender community who are able to voice their objection to this asserted manifesto, and who openly state that they welcome different treatment options, rather than a one-solution-fits-all approach. This would leave many, for whom sex-reassignment is not an option, without any help at all.

SHOULD TRANSGENDER PEOPLE ONLY BE TREATED BY PROFESSIONALS WHO ARE TRANSGENDER THEMSELVES?

Another familiar argument put forward by some transgender political activists is that transgender persons should only be treated by health professionals who are, themselves, transgender. The premise of such an argument is that one would need to experience a condition first-hand to be able to understand, and thus be in a position to help.

The problem with this argument is that, as I have hopefully conveyed so far in this book, gender dysphoria is a broad category of many different gender identity presentations. There is a danger in assuming that all people with gender dysphoria are the same, as this is evidently not accurate. As such it would be impossible for a trained health professional to have every conceivable type of gender dysphoria themselves. It is also a rather simplistic premise to assume that understanding may not be achieved without first-hand experience. If that was the case, all gynaecologists would have to be women, and most psychiatrists would have to have experienced a psychosis. That being said, the specialist gender dysphoria psychotherapy, as I have outlined in this book, takes the form of a small therapy group, consisting of a therapist and up to eight members with gender dysphoria. As described elsewhere in this book, the modified mentalisation-based group-analytic therapy is delivered in the group by the whole group, not just by the therapist alone. As such, the people with gender dysphoria within the group form the thinking and working group collaboratively with the therapist. And so, whilst the therapist may not themselves have gender dysphoria, the therapy is being delivered by the working group, the majority of whom do have a gender dysphoria.

SHOULD GENDER DYSPHORIA BE CONSIDERED A MENTAL DISORDER?

The inclusion of gender dysphoria within the classification systems used in psychiatry, namely the DSM and ICD, remains controversial within the transgender community. (I am using the term 'community' because it is already in use, and as such, giving it validity even though, as mentioned earlier, I am none too clear who the 'community' is). One proposed argument is that the person with a transgender identity may perceive their problem as a physical issue, not a mental issue, and that, to classify them as having a mental disorder is stigmatising. Others argue that it should not be considered a disorder of the mind or body.

On the other hand, there are also arguments for gender dysphoria to remain in the psychiatric classification systems. It could be argued that, as there is no actual physical problem or pathology located in the body, it is the conflict with their discordant sense of psychological gender that causes the distress, and that's the reason the person seeks professional help. It is the psychological distress, which would warrant it being retained as a mental disorder.

If gender dysphoria was not considered either a mental or physical disorder then it would be very difficult for the persons to access any help or interventions from health professionals including doctors, psychologists or surgeons. In many parts of the world a diagnosis or recognised 'condition' with a corresponding classification code may be required in order to obtain any psychological, medical or surgical help or intervention.

Of course, being subversively creative regarding one's sense of gender in an individual way does not imply a disorder. A person who is confident in their own sense of gender, and who is able to play with societal gender frameworks, without feeling uncomfortable, unstable or uncertain about their own sense of gender identity, and doesn't experience any mental confusion or disturbance, would not be considered to suffer from a mental disorder. Similarly, a person whose gender did not fit within a societally normative or binary gender framework should probably not be considered to be suffering from a mental disorder. A person who was uncertain, confused, unhappy, or distressed about their sense of gender identity may however be considered as suffering from a gender identity disorder.

THE EMPEROR'S NEW CLOTHES?

Early in my career when I was a specialist registrar training at The Portman Clinic I gave a lecture, 'Transsexualism: a case of the emperor's new clothes?' which appeared a number of years later as a chapter in a psychoanalytic lecture series book. In the paper, I ask a number of questions relating to how psychiatry considers transsexualism as a condition. The paper proved to be controversial within some quarters of a vocal trans activist political community for reasons I will now describe:

One part of the paper asked the question: why is the belief that one is the opposite gender not classified in psychiatry as a delusional belief? Rather than making the claim that transsexuals were psychotic, I was asking the question from a phenomenological perspective. In psychiatry, a firmly held, false belief is termed a delusion. If a person held the belief that they were actually a different species of animal, or a different person to whom they were, or indeed had any characteristics which they did not have, then this would fulfil the criteria for a delusional belief. It was on this premise that I was enquiring as to why it was then, when a person had the belief that they were the opposite sex or gender, that psychiatry was not classifying this as a delusion? After all, if I believed I was a goldfish I would be delusional. If I believed I was a tree I would be delusional. If I believed I actually belonged to a different ethnic or racial category, I would be delusional.

So if I believed I was a different sex to the one I had would that not make me delusional?

The answer to this question is that it is not a delusional belief, as the majority of transgender people wanting gender reassignment do not believe that they *are already* the preferred gender. They believe that they *should be*, or *would like* to be the preferred gender. It is this distinction, which qualitatively distinguishes the characteristics of this conviction from that of a delusion. If the person was to instead believe that they were already the preferred gender, then presumably they would not be pursuing sex reassignment as there would be no need. In the several years of assessing people with gender dysphoria, I have heard many people initially make the statement that they believe that they are of the opposite gender to their biological sex. But upon further enquiry, the majority will concede that it is rather the conviction that they *should be*, or *should have been*, or *would like to become* a member of the opposite gender rather than already occupying that gender status. As such this does not constitute a delusion and people with gender dysphoria are not psychotic.

The other section of the paper described the discrepancy at times between the apparent and acknowledged gender perceptions people may admit to. At times this may be in conflict with the actual perceptions of a person's gender. Patients of mine have reported how, whilst they have an idea of how they perceive themselves in terms of gender, it has been difficult for some to ascertain exactly how others perceive them in terms of gender. They have described how people have been careful to say the right things to them and treat them in accordance with their newly acquired gender, while still being left uncertain as to how they were actually being perceived beyond the polite civility on the surface. This is where the analogy to the Hans Christian Anderson story of *The Emperor's New Clothes* came in. It was the impolite child in the civilised society who was able to offer the Emperor an honest account of how he perceived him. In the original paper, I speculated that perhaps it was the role of the psychoanalytic psychotherapist to take on the position of the honest boy in the story. However, I have since revised this opinion several years down the line, having modified both my understanding of the condition and the modality of my therapeutic delivery.

Over the many years of working with gender dysphoric persons I came to understand that the therapist is not in a position to offer an account to the patient as to how they perceive them in terms of their gender. Indeed, the therapist's account should not be of any particular standing. The role of the therapist is to assist the patient in acquiring the skills to gain as much of an objective perspective on themselves as possible. This is a skill, which is developed through the process of the therapy and not merely provided for by the therapist. The working of a therapeutic group, as described earlier in this book, provides a useful therapeutic mechanism whereby such objective perspectives may be gleaned from fellow patients in the group and used to inform one's own perspective of oneself. Returning to the original story of *The Emperor's New Clothes*, it will not come as a surprise that one of my patients who was concerned as to how 'passable' she really was as a woman, resorted to walking outside secondary schools around closing time. She knew that if the children did not perceive her as convincingly female, they would not hesitate in letting her know in a very uncivilised manner. Needless to say, this particular patient also had some accompanying masochistic tendencies.

THE ROYAL COLLEGE OF PSYCHIATRISTS: TIME TO CHANGE CONFERENCE MAY 2011

In May 2011, The Royal College of Psychiatrists were due to host a small conference with a number of speakers delivering lectures on gender dysphoria. The invited speakers came from differing backgrounds, each with differing perspectives: spanning psychiatry, with representatives from the Charing Cross Gender Identity Clinic in London, myself representing a dedicated specialist gender dysphoria psychotherapy service, a child psychiatrist, representing child and adolescent gender services, and the feminist journalist, Julie Bindel. The conference was scheduled as a one-day meeting, with each of the speakers giving a presentation followed by a discussion between the gathered panel of speakers and the audience. The planned event was billed by the Royal College as '*an extremely stimulating meeting exploring the most recent academic, clinical and contemporary thinking on transgender issues, for all people interested in this field*'.

There was nothing particularly controversial about the meeting. There were no changes being proposed to public policies or legislature. There were no new guidelines for treatment or any diagnostic criteria. It was quite simply scheduled to be a rare gathering of people in the UK who were already working and publishing within the field of gender dysphoria, all coming together for an exchange of ideas in a professional environment, much the same as may occur with professionals working with any particular branch of medicine, psychiatry or psychology. However, shortly after the scheduled meeting was advertised there was uproar within a small section of the trans activist community.

A small number of politically motivated trans activists took great offence that the Royal College was hosting a meeting of professionals, and especially enraged that certain speakers had been invited. There appeared to be uproar aimed at all the speakers for some politically motivated reason or another, and in my case, the outrage was that I was offering a dedicated psychotherapy service for people with gender dysphoria. The reality of the service I offer is, as described earlier in this book: a dedicated psychotherapy service for people with a variety of gender identity conditions which is completely complementary to any physical sex reassignment they may be undergoing. One of the reasons for the service is that gender dysphoria is outside of the realm of experience of most psychotherapists who may be in danger of over-attending to the gender dysphoria, under-attending it, or just not knowing how to attend to it. However, the very vocal trans activists incorrectly presumed that anyone offering psychotherapy to people with gender dysphoria must surely be trying to 'cure them' of their transgender in the way that some psychotherapists may have attempted to 'cure' homosexuals of their sexuality some decades ago.

The trans activists posted on websites, blogged furiously (in both *vigour and content*) and urged transgender people to stage a protest. It is unclear what the protest was about, as they would have had no idea what any of the proposed speakers would have said – no abstracts had been submitted to the conference organisers at that point. The protest appeared to be raising objection to the very idea that professionals were going to be allowed to think about gender dysphoria at all. Misinformed presumptions about the speakers, including myself, were virally distributed on the internet, and descended into personalised attacks. At one stage I was literally being demonised; one trans activist blogged that he / she thought my eyes made me look like the devil. Patients in therapy at the time were both confused by the very personal vitriol, as the transphobic demon being purported on the net didn't bear any resemblance to the therapist sat in front of them. Some were tempted to respond to the chaos, but most were able to distance themselves from what they perceived as a politically driven and seemingly paranoid minority.

The main objection raised by some sectors within the trans activist political community was that the Royal College of Psychiatrists was looking at opening up debate. There was a suggestion that psychiatrists were perhaps not allowed to think, or enquire about the condition at all. Of course, it would be a very unfortunate day if psychiatrists were no longer able to think, enquire, question, or open up a debate about any of the conditions they treated. If this was the case, there would of course be no research, no progress and no development in understanding.

The most extreme activists suggested that not only were psychiatrists not supposed to think about the condition, but that their role was only limited to providing cross-sex hormones and giving the go-ahead for sex reassignment. This of course would defeat the purpose of being a psychiatrist and do a disservice to the very many patients with gender dysphoria who benefit greatly from having a psychiatrist think with them. It also presumes that all people with a gender dysphoria are transsexual and all the same as each other. It ignores the very many people with gender identity conditions other than transsexuality, and for whom physical sex-reassignment interventions are not an appropriate option.

In the weeks coming up to the event, the politically driven trans activists managed to drum up enough protesters who were threatening violent action at the meeting that the Royal College decided to cancel it. This was undoubtedly seen as a victory for the political trans activists, but, as a great deal of transgender people have since vocalised, it was a huge disappointment for many people within the transgender community. It is rare, in fact almost unheard of, for a variety of professionals with differing backgrounds to come together in the UK to think usefully about gender dysphoria (which makes us very different from other countries where gender services are very open and inclusive). And on this occasion, it was members of the transgender community itself who put a stop to it. Since the cancellation of the conference, many members of the transgender community have articulated their disappointment, and their sense of being unfairly represented by the small trans activist lobby, whose political aim was for all people with gender identity conditions to be considered the same: for them all to be considered transsexual, all to be given sex reassignment, and for none of them to be thought about, especially by professionals who had not had sex changes themselves.

The reality is that whilst there are a small number of health professionals who dedicate their professional careers to the field of gender dysphoria, and find the work rewarding, there are a great many others who are put off working in the field due to the challenging responses they frequently experience from some trans activists.

QUEENSLAND TRANSGENDER, SISTERGIRL & GENDER DIVERSE CONFERENCE, AUSTRALIA 2012

A year later from the cancelled UK Royal College of Psychiatrists conference and on the other side of the world, a similar conference was being organised in Queensland, Australia. The Queensland Transgender, Sistergirl and Gender Diverse conference was to be the first of its kind in Australia, open to both professionals and the public, with psychiatrists, psychotherapists, psychologists, surgeons, trans activists, and gender diverse people themselves all in attendance.

I was invited as a keynote speaker to present a paper outlining my specialist gender dysphoria psychotherapy service as described earlier in this book. As predicted, the trans activist minority who had been so vocal around the time of the proposed London conference, resurfaced and aimed their campaign to the organisers seeking that the conference should be cancelled, or some of the proposed speakers should be uninvited. Unlike London, where the organisers decided to cancel the conference, the organisers of the Queensland conference chose a different response. Perhaps in true determined Aussie style, the organisers stuck to their proposed list of speakers rather than give in to the protesters' demands or threats.

The conference went ahead as planned in Cairns, August 2012, and received more than three times the anticipated attendance.

The conference was a great success, and much credit was rightly given to the disciplined and courageous organisers, co-ordinated by Professor Darren Russell.

Surgeons from Thailand delivered lectures alongside GPs, counsellors, and hormone prescribing psychiatrists. Professor Milton Diamond presented an overview of his work as a sexologist, and I talked about gender identity psychotherapy. Unsurprisingly, there didn't appear to be any controversy from my presentation on psychotherapy (I clearly was not the evil demon some of the trans activists had feared, or perhaps hoped I would be). In addition to the professionals, the conference gathered representatives from a variety of service-user organisations from the transgender and intersex communities.

The conference was both informative and touching in many ways. It was the first time that a co-ordinated dialogue between a variety of professionals and transgender service users had taken place within Australia at a dedicated conference. Given that the conference was in Australia, it was only right that there was also a symposium dedicated to 'Sistergirls' who are the male-to-female transgender component of the indigenous Aboriginal population in Australia, many of whom had never met another sistergirl prior to the conference. The Cairns conference attempted and succeeded in doing what the London conference had set out to do and became a milestone conference, paving the way for successive similar transgender conferences in Australia.

From the conference, I was pleased to meet the trans activist Melissa Vick who has remained a friend and we have enjoyed catch-up dinners and stimulating discussions on both sides of the world since. I am grateful to her for her contributions to this book.

For an alternative perspective from a feminist perspective I guide the reader to the writings of Sheila Jeffreys, especially her book, 'Gender Hurts' – a book a transgender patient of mine recommended to me as one which they had found especially helpful. That may come as a surprise to many trans activists who take issue with her writings.

A couple of years ago, I met with a couple of people who worked for a well-known transgender charity. I wanted to take time to meet them and let them know about a gender dysphoria therapy service I was setting up. When we met they seemed less interested in the actual specialist therapy service, and their questions focused on why I was not prescribing cross-sex hormones. I pointed out repeatedly that my work has only ever been in psychotherapy for gender dysphoria, and I was unique as the only consultant psychiatrist in the UK (to my knowledge) specialising in the assessment, psychotherapeutic treatment and research into this area, compared with the numerous clinicians who are more experienced in prescribing hormones; something I have no experience of. Their persistence was striking but the meeting was still pleasant enough, and I hoped that it could lead to some helpful collaborative work together. Some days after our meeting, they emailed to advise me that they realised I was the same person who some vocal trans activists had been unhappy about some years before, due to a psychoanalytically orientated paper I had written earlier in my career. I pointed out that in the years since then, I had written several subsequent papers detailing revisions of my ideas and understanding of the condition, and that this was also clearly stated on the gender dysphoria pages of my professional website just to make it very clear. The reply they gave me was that *'transgender people have very long memories, and as such, it is difficult for them to change how they perceive someone.'* They suggested that, because of that, they would not be willing to work collaboratively with me for fear of association. I found this response to be surprising and strikingly relevant. A strong fear I have observed in some, but by no means all transgender people relates to whether others will be able to accept them in their new post-transition gender, or whether others will continue to identify them and refer to them in the previous gender which they no longer identify themselves in. The notion I was being presented: that transgender people would not be able to accept a shift in an academic professional's theoretical understanding, or perceive them any differently, despite a stated change on the part of the professional seemed especially poignant, albeit somewhat ironic.

AFTERWORD

 Az Hakeem: This book has been a labour of love, and I hope you found it helpful, informative, and thought-provoking. Perhaps it has even challenged the way you think about gender, transgender, and gender dysphoria.

As you'll have gathered from what we've written, anyone who publishes ideas and opinions in the field of transgender are at risk of someone, somewhere, disagreeing and possibly being offended if the proposed ideas don't match their own. There will always be many varied ideas, but this book was not simply one based on my own ideas alone. In fact, the content has been informed by the hundreds of transgender people I have seen in my professional work, and those known to my colleagues who have also contributed chapters, some of whom are themselves trans. I am indebted to good friend, Sarah who is a trans woman, who was extremely helpful in assisting in the proof-editing of the text and whose input has been invaluable. This is not a book written by a cis person from a cis-perspective but a collaborative effort of many people both 'trans' and 'cis' (if you aren't familiar with the term 'cis' then you've obviously skipped a chapter or two!).

My attempt was to condense as much of what I have learned and experienced from my specialist work and research over the years into a book which could be helpful to anyone and everyone. Whilst I wanted to provide a whistle-stop tour of everything trans, I also wanted to get the balance between providing enough detail, and writing so much that the book would be too big for anyone to read.

When teaching students, I tell them that the 'take home message' if they forget all else, is that they need to question everything in order to get a greater understanding of it. This also applies to gender: what they understand gender to be or to mean, and what they presume others to understand by it. I encourage them to deconstruct any assumptions they have regarding gender and to question any 'default' presumptions or associations they have with gender, masculinity, femininity, or what it means to be male, female, trans or any other gender identity.

Hopefully through this book I have invited you as the reader to question what it means to be male, female, trans, or any other gender. Hopefully by now you will have appreciated that transgender is not a phenomenon which is the same in everyone trans, but that there are many differing types of transgender or gender dysphoria and that a 'one-solution fits all' is by no means a satisfactory approach. All too frequently the focus is on the body of the trans person, but as a psychiatrist and psychotherapist, my aim with this book has been to consider the psychology of trans and the emotional and mental impact transgender has on the trans person, their families and those around them.

I am grateful to many colleagues who have contributed chapters to TRANS. I am hugely indebted to Fintan Harte for welcoming me into the body of specialists in gender dysphoria in Australia and New Zealand (ANZPATH) and for being such a wonderful friend in addition to his substantial contribution to this book and my research. Valsa Eapen, Rudi Crncec, and Mona Asghari-Fard, are my research team at UNSW. Despite being on the other side of the world, they were extremely helpful in their collaboration, resulting in the creation of the GPSQ.

I am grateful to my school-friend Helen who gave me advice on how to go about putting my writing into print, and to Jane who helped me through the process of doing this. I am immensely grateful to The Shaw Mind Foundation who asked me to be their professional patron, a position of which I am extremely proud, and to Trigger Press, for agreeing to publish this book and for their patience with me!

The aim of the Shaw Mind Foundation is to raise awareness and reduce stigma in relation to mental health conditions. As a psychiatrist, my aim is for everyone to be happy in their life and to be psychologically well informed about it. I also see it as my role to question and challenge assumptions, presumptions with the ultimate aim of furthering our understanding of ourselves. As a doctor and a scientist, I realise we will never know all there is to know, but as the phrase goes, 'knowledge is power'. The more we can understand about what happens in our minds, then the more empowered we will be to deal with whatever life throws at us.

APPENDIX

1. Diagnostic and Statistical Manual of Mental Disorders,
   Fifth Edition (DSM-5).

   by American Psychiatric Association (Author).

2. ICD-10: The ICD-10 Classification of Mental and Behavioural
   Disorders: Clinical Descriptions and Diagnostic Guidelines.

   by World Health Organization (Contributor) (1992).

3. Gender Preoccupation and Stability Questionnaire (GPSQ).

GPSQ: GENDER PREOCCUPATION AND STABILITY QUESTIONNAIRE

i) **Today's date:** _____

ii) **Your name:** _____

iii) **Your age (in years):** _____

iv) **Biological sex assigned to you at birth** (please circle one):
male / female / intersex

v) **Current gender** (please circle one):
male / female / intersex / transgender male / transgender female / transgender (unspecified) / gender queer / gender neutral / other (specify):

vi) **Do you feel confident that you will be able to lead a satisfied life with whatever gender identity you feel that you currently have?** (please circle one):
Extremely confident / confident / somewhat confident / not very confident / not at all confident

The GPSQ consists of 14 questions relating to your thoughts and feelings about gender, including your own sense of gender identity. Gender refers to whatever gender you identify as yourself (e.g. masculine, feminine, transgender, gender-queer or other gender variants) which may or may not be the same as your biological sex.

When answering these questions, please circle the answer that best reflects your thoughts and feelings **over the past 2 weeks.**

1. **How important do you feel gender is to you?**
   a) unimportant
   b) slightly important
   c) moderately important
   d) very important
   e) extremely important

2. **In the past 2 weeks how often have you thought about gender?**
   a) never
   b) seldom
   c) sometimes
   d) often
   e) very often

3. **In the past two weeks how often have you given consideration to gender in relation to aspects of your day-to-day life such as work, recreational activities or products purchased?**

   a) never
   b) seldom
   c) sometimes
   d) often
   e) very often

4. **In the past 2 weeks how troubled have you been about issues relating to gender?**

   a) never
   b) seldom
   c) sometimes
   d) often
   e) very often

5. **In the past 2 weeks have you stopped yourself from participating in any activity, behaving in a certain way or purchasing anything because of your gender?**

   a) never
   b) seldom
   c) sometimes
   d) often
   e) very often

6. **In the past 2 weeks has it upset you when you have had to answer questions about what sex or gender you are (e.g. when filling in forms)?**

   a) never
   b) seldom
   c) sometimes
   d) often
   e) very often

7. **In the past 2 weeks how comfortable have you felt with your sense of gender?** (this does not have to correspond with your biological sex)

   a) extremely comfortable
   b) very comfortable
   c) somewhat comfortable
   d) not very comfortable
   e) not comfortable at all

8. **In the past 2 weeks have you felt uncertain or confused about your sense of gender?**
   a) never
   b) seldom
   c) sometimes
   d) often
   e) very often

9. **In the past 2 weeks have you felt pressured to behave or act in certain ways because of gender?**
   a) not at all
   b) hardly ever
   c) sometimes
   d) often
   e) all the time

10. **In the past two weeks has your sense of what gender you identify with changed at all?**
    a) not at all
    b) hardly ever
    c) sometimes
    d) often
    e) all the time

11. **In the past 2 weeks have you avoided social situations because of uncertainties or anxieties you have about your sense of your own identity?**
    a) not at all
    b) hardly ever
    c) sometimes
    d) often
    e) all the time

12. **In the past 2 weeks have you had thoughts that you should change your sex (even if you have already changed your sex in the past)?**
    a) not at all
    b) hardly ever
    c) sometimes
    d) often
    e) all the time

13. **In the past 2 weeks has your sense of what gender you are changed from one day to the next?**
    a) not at all
    b) hardly ever
    c) sometimes
    d) often
    e) all the time

14. **In the past 2 weeks have you had any thoughts that you needed to seek professional help in order to change the physical sex of your body?**

a) not at all

b) hardly ever

c) sometimes

d) often

e) all the time

GUIDE TO USING THE GPSQ

There are 14 questions, which are scored in the GPSQ.

For each question on the GPSQ the responses are scored as follows:

(a) = 1

(b) = 2

(c) = 3

(d) = 4

(e) = 5

The total score range is 14–70

The GPSQ may be used to measure the following:

- The extent of Gender Dysphoria
- Change of severity of Gender Dysphoria

As such, the GPSQ may be used to measure the effectiveness of any clinical intervention aimed at lessening Gender Dysphoria (such as psychological, hormonal, surgical, etc.)

Total scores equal or greater than 28 are highly suggestive of Gender Dysphoria.

A change in GPSQ total score by 11 points or more reliably indicates a change in the degree of Gender Dysphoria.

When the total score drops by 11 points or more but remains at or above 28 then this is evidence of a lessening of Gender Dysphoria but still within the clinical range highly suggestive for Gender Dysphoria.

If the total score falls below 28 then that person may be considered to no longer clinically have a Gender Dysphoria.

Reproductions of this scale must include the full scale title and reference and no alterations.

Reference: Hakeem A; Crncec R; Asghari-Fard M; Harte F; Eapen V. Development and Validation of a measure for assessing gender dysphoria in adults: The Gender Preoccupation and Stability Questionnaire (GPSQ). *International Journal of Transgenderism* (in press) 2016.

REFERENCES

About a girl. *Australian Story*. 15 August 2016.
http://www.abc.net.au/austory/content/2016/s4515697.htm

American Psychiatric Association. (2013). *Diagnostic and Statistical Manual of Mental Disorders* (5th ed.). Washington, DC: Author.

Anthony W. Bateman & Peter Fonagy. (2004). *Mentalization-Based Treatment of BPD. Journal of Personality Disorders*. Vol. 18, No. 1, 36–51.

ANZCOG Male to female transsexualism. (2006). (Word document) www.menopause.com.au/announce.asp. Laparoscopic pelvic floor repair of prolapsed neovagina. Australian and New Zealand Journal of Obstetrics and Gynaecology. 46: 254–260.

Being Me. *4 Corners*. Australian Broadcasting Commission, 17 November 2014. www.abc.net.au/4corners/stories/2014/11/17/4127631.htm

Bauer, G., Hammond, R., Travers, R., Kaay, M., Hohenadel, K. & Boyce, M. (2010). 'I don't think this is theoretical; this is our lives': How erasure impacts health care for transgender people. *Journal of the Association of Nurses in AIDS Care*. 20. 348–61.

Beyondblue. *The First Australian National Trans Mental Health Study, Summary of Results* www.beyondblue.org.au/docs/default-source/research-project-files/bw0288_the-first-australian-national-trans-mental-health-study---summary-of-results.pdf?sfvrsn=2

Blanchard, R. (1989). *The concept of autogynephilia and the typology of male gender dysphoria*. The Journal of Nervous and Mental Disease. 177, (10), 616–23.

Bockting, W. & Coleman, E. (1992). *A comprehensive approach to the treatment of gender dysphoria. in Gender dysphoria*. Journal of Psychology and Human Sexuality. 5(4), 131–55.

Brill, S. & Pepper, R. (2008). *The transgender child: A handbook for families and professionals.* San Fransisco, CA: Cleis Press Inc.

Brock, L. L., Nishida, T. K., Chiong, C., Grimm, K. J. & Rimm-Kaufman, S. E. (2008). *Children's perceptions of the classroom environment and social and academic performance: A longitudinal analysis of the contribution of the Responsive Classroom approach*. Journal of School Psychology, 46(2), 129–49.

Bullough, B. & Bullough, V. (1998). *Transsexualism: Historical perspectives, 1952 to present.* In D. Denny (Ed.), Current concepts in transgender identity. New York: Garland.

Call me Cate. *Australian Story.* 24 Feb 2014. Video no longer available; transcript at http://www.abc.net.au/austory/content/2012/s3951204.htm

Chodorow, N. J. (1995). *Gender as a Personal and Cultural Construction.* Signs. 20(3), 516–44.

Coleman, E., Bockting, W., Botzer, M., Cohen-Kettenis, P., DeCuypere, G., Feldman, J., Fraser, L., Green, J., Knudson, G., Meyer, W.J., Monstrey, S., Adler, R.K., Brown, G.R., Devor, A.H., Ehrbar, R., Ettner, R., Eyler, E., Garofalo, R., Karasic, D.H., Lev, A.I., Mayer, G., Meyer-Bahlburg, H., Hall, B.P., Pfaefflin, F., Rachlin, K., Robinson, B., Schechter, L.S., Tangpricha, V., van Trotsenburg, M., Vitale, A., Winter, S., Whittle, S., Wylie, K.R. & Zucker, K. (2012). *Standards of Care for the Health of Transsexual, Transgender, and Gender-Nonconforming People.* Version 7. International Journal of Transgenderism. 13(4), 165–232.

Connell, R. (2012). *Transsexual women and feminist thought: Toward new understanding and new politics.* Signs, 37(4), 857–81.

Coolidge, F., These. L. & Youn. S. (2002). *The heritability of gender identity disorder in a child and adolescent twin sample.* Behavior Genetics, 32, 251–57.

Couric, K. *Interview with Carmen Carrera and Laverne Cox.* Unable to locate original interview but the critical Cox comments are at www.youtube.com/watch?v=sMH8FH7O9xA; a commentary on the interview can be found at www.salon.com/2014/01/07/laverne_cox_artfully_shuts_down_katie_courics_invasive_questions_about_transgender_people/.

Crenshaw, K. (1991). *Mapping the margins: Intersectionality, identity politics and violence against women of color.* Stanford Law Review, 43(6), 1241–99.

Deogracis, J. J., Johnson, L. L., Meyer-Bahlburg, H. F., Kessler, S. J., Schober, J. M. & Zucker, K. J. (2007). *The gender identity/ gender dysphoria questionnaire for adolescents and adults. Journal of sex research.* 44 (4), 370–79.

Dhejne C. et al. (2011). *Long-Term Follow-Up of Transsexual Persons Undergoing Sex Reassignment Surgery: Cohort Study in Sweden.* PLoS ONE, Volume 6 / Issue 2.

Diamond, M. (1965). *A critical evaluation of the ontogeny of human sexual behaviour. The Quarterly Review of Biology:* Vol 40, No. 2 June.

Diamond, M. (2006). *Biased-interaction theory of psychosexual development: 'how does one know if one is male or female?'.* Sex Roles 55: 589–600.

Diamond, M. (2012). *Intersex and Transsex: atypical gender development and social construction.* Women's studies review 19:76-91.

Diamond, M. (2013). *Transsexuality among twins: Identity concordance, transition, rearing, and orientation.* International Journal of Transgenderism. 14(1), 24–38.

Eden, K., Wylie, K. & Watson, E. (2012). *Gender dysphoria: recognition and assessment.* Advances in Psychiatric Treatment. 18(1) 2–11.

Emerson, S. & Rosenfeld, C. (1996). *Stages of Adjustment in Family Members of Transgender Individuals.* Journal of Family Psychotherapy. 7(3), 1–12.

English, B. *Led by the child who simply knew.* Boston Globe, 11 December 2011. www.bostonglobe.com/metro/2011/12/11/led-child-who-simply-knew/SsH1U9Pn9JKArTiumZdxaL/story.html

Erasmus, J., Bagga, H. & Harte, F. (2015). *Assessing patient satisfaction with a multidisciplinary gender dysphoria clinic in Melbourne.* Australasian Psychiatry. Vol 23(2) 158–162.

Ettner, R. (1999). *Gender loving care: A guide to counseling gender-variant clients.* New York, NY: W.W. Norton & Company, Inc.

Fonagy, P. & Target, M. (1998). *Mentalization and the Changing Aims of Child Psychoanalysis. Psychoanalytic Dialogues: The International Journal of Relational Perspectives* 8(1), 87-114.

Foulkes, S. H. (1983). *Introduction to Group-Analytic Psychotherapy: Studies in the Social Integration of Individuals and Groups.* Maresfield Reprints.

Freeland, S. (Director). (2013). *Her Story* (web-based mini series). www.herstoryshow.com.

Gender Recognition Act (2004). www.legislation.gov.uk

Goldner, V. (1991). *Toward a Critical Relational Theory of Gender. Psychoanalytic Dialogues: The International Journal of Relational Perspectives.* 1, 249–72.

Graham, J. E. (2011). *Bullying and childhood abuse: Implications for mental and physical health across the lifespan.* Paper presented at the WPATH 2011 Biennial International Symposium: Transgender Beyond Disorder: Identity, Community, and Health, Emory Conference Center, Atlanta, Georgia.

Gray, S., Carter, A. & Levitt, H. (2012). *A critical review of assumptions about gender variant children in psychological research.* Journal of Gay & Lesbian Mental Health, 16(1), 4–30.

Hakeem, A. (2006). *Transsexualism: a case of The Emperor's New Clothes?* Lectures on Violence Perversion and Delinquency. Edited by Morgan, D and Ruscynzski, S. Chapter 10. Karnac Books.

Hakeem, A. (2010). *Parallel Processes: observed in the patient, therapy and organisation.* Group Analysis. The International Journal of Group Analysis 43(4).

Hakeem, A. (2012). *Psychotherapy for Gender Identity Disorders. Advances in Psychiatric Treatment.* Vol.18, 17–24.

Hakeem, A., Eapen, V., Crncec, R., Asghari-Fard, M. & Harte, F. (2016). *Development and validation of a measure for assessing gender dysphoria in adults: The Gender Preoccupation and Stability Questionnaire.* Submitted for publication at time of writing.

Hammond, R. *The Social Organisation of Health Care for Trans Youth in Ontario.* Master's Thesis, Dalhousie University, Halifax, Nova Scotia.

Hegedus, J. (2009). *When a daughter becomes a son: Parents' acceptance of their transgender children.* In partial fulfillment of the requirements of the degree doctor of psychology, Alliant International University, San Francisco Campus.

Hembree, W.C., Cohen-Kettenis, P., Delemarre-van de Waal, H.A., Gooren, L.J., Meyer, W.J., Spack, N.P., Tangpricha, V. & Montori, V.M. *Endocrine Treatment of Transsexual Persons: An Endocrine Society Clinical Practice Guideline.* Journal of Clinical and Endocrinology Metabolism 2009; 94, 3132-3154van de Ven, B. F. M. L. (2008). Facial feminisation, why and how? Sexologies. 17(4), 291–98.

Herdt, G. (1994). *Third sex, third gender: Beyond sexual dimorphism in culture and history.* New York: Zone Books.

Hyde, Z., Doherty, M., Tilley, M., McCaul, K., Rooney, R. & Jance, J. (2014). *The First Australian National Trans Mental Health Study: Summary of Results.* Perth, Australia: School of Public Health, Curtin University.

Hyde, S. (Director). (2013). *52 Tuesdays* (feature film), Closer Productions. Adelaide. www.closerproductions.com.au/films/52-tuesdays.

Jeffreys, S. (2014). *Gender Hurts: A feminist analysis of the politics of trasnsgenderism.* Routledge.

Kadushin, G. (1996). *Gay Men with Aids and Their Families of Origin: An Analysis of Social Support.* Health and Social Work. 21(2),141–49.

Krieger, I. (2011). *Helping your transgender teen: A guide for parents.* New Haven: Genderwise Press.

Lesser, J. (1999). *When Your Son Becomes Your Daughter: A Parent's Adjustment to a Transgender Child.* Families in Society. 80(2), 182–89.

Lev, A. (2004). *Transgender emergence: Therapeutic guidelines for working with gender-variant people and their families.* Binghamton, NY: Haworth.

McGuire, J. K., Anderson, C. R., Toomey, R. B. & Russell, S. T. (2010). *School climate for transgender youth: a mixed method investigation of student experiences and school responses.* Journal of Youth and Adolescence. 39, 1175–88.

McWilliams, N. (1999). *Psychoanalytic Case Formulations.* New York: Guilford Publications.

Money, J. & Anke Ehrhardt. (1996). *Man & Woman, Boy & Girl: Gender Identity from Conception to Maturity.* Northvale, N.J.: Jason Aronson.

Namaste, V. (2000). *Invisible Lives: The Erasure of Transsexual and Transgender People.* Chicago, University of Chicago Press.

Newbury, P. (2011) *Harmful ubiquity: introducing Cisnormativity.* https://cisnormativity.wor press.com/2011/08/23/harmful-ubiquity-introducing-cisnormativity/;

Olson, K.R., Durwood, L., DeMeules, M. & McLaughlin K.A. (2016). *Mental Health of Transgender Children Who Are Supported in Their Identities.* Pediatric. 137(3).

O'Reilly, S. (2012). *Shunning Medical Hoops, Transgender Patients Turn to 'Informed Consent' Model.* http://genprogress.org/voices/2012/02/28/17609/shunningmedical-hoops-transgender-patients-turn-to-informed-consent-m/

Parker, R. (1995). *Parent Love/Parent Hate: The Power of Maternal Ambivalence.* New York: Basic Books.

Pearlman, S. F. (2006). *Terms of connection: Mother-talk about female-to-male transgender children.* In J. Bigner & A. Gottlieb (Eds.). Interventions with families of gay, lesbian, bisexual and transgender people: From the inside out. Binghamton, New York: Harrington Park Press.

Pyne, J. (2011). *Unsuitable bodies: Trans people and cisnormativity in shelter services.* Canadian Social Work Review. 28(1), 129.

Queensland Transgender, Sistergirl, and Gender Diverse Conference. *Health and Well-being into the Future.* 24-25th August 2012, Cairns. www.transconference.org.au

Riley, E. A., Sitharthan, G., Clemso, L. & Diamond, M. (2011). *The Needs of Gender-Variant Children and Their Parents: A Parent Survey.* International Journal of Sexual Health. 23, 181–95.

Riley, E. A., Clemson, L., Sitharthan, G. & Diamond, M. (2013). *Surviving a gender variant childhood: The views of transgender adults on the needs of gender variant children and their parents.* Journal of Sex & Marital Therapy, 39(3), 241–263. doi:10.1080/0092623X.2011.628439

Rutter, M. (1987). Psychosocial Resilience and Protective Mechanisms. American Journal of Orthopsychiatry 57(3), 316–31.

Safe Schools Coalition Australia (SSCA) www.safeschoolscoalition.org.au

Sam and Evan (2011). *From Girls to Men.* Nine Lives Media.

Scheinfeld, A. (1944). *Women and men.* New York: Harcourt, Brace and Co.

Serano, J. (2007). *Whipping Girl: A Transsexual Woman on Sexism and the Scapegoating of Femininity.* Berkeley, Seal Press.

Spade, D. (2011). *Normal Life: Administrative Violence, Critical Trans Politics, and the Limits of Law.* Brooklyn, South End Press.

Smith, M. & Payne, M. (2015). *Bullying, Binaries, Bathrooms, and Biology: Conversations with Elementary Educators about Supporting Transgender Students.* Gender and Education Conference. Queering Education Research Institute. London, UK.

Stoller, R. (1968). *Sex and Gender: On the Development of Masculinity and Femininity.* Science House, New York City.

Stoller, R. (1968). *Sex and Gender:* Vol 2: The Transsexual Experiment. Hogarth.

Stoller, R. (1975). *Perversion: The Erotic Form of Hatre.* Pantheon, New York.

Stufft, D. L. & Graff, C. M. (2011). *Increasing visibility for LGBTQ students: What schools can do to create inclusive classroom communities.* Current Issues in Education. 14(1), 1–24.

Stulberg, I. & Buckingham, S. (1988). *Parallel Issues for Aids Patients, Families and Others.* Social Casework, 355, 59.

WHO – World Health Organisation. (1999). *International Classification of Diseases Tenth Revision.*

Winter, S., Diamond, M., Green, J., Karasic, D., Reed, T., Whittle, S. & Wylie K. (2016). *Transgender people: health at the margins of society.* The Lancet 388 (10042), 390–400.

Winter, S., Settle, E., Wylie, K., Reisner, S., Cabral, M., Knudson, G. & Baral, S. (2016). *Synergies in health and human rights: a call to action to improve transgender health.* Lancet. 388(10042): 318–21.

Wylie, K., Eden, K., & Watson, E. (2012). *Gender dysphoria: treatment and outcomes.* Advances in Psychiatric Treatment. 18 (1), 12–16.

Wylie, K., Knudson, G., Khan, S.I., Bonierbale, M., Wayanyusakal, S. & Baral, S. (2016). *Serving Transgender People: Clinical Care Considerations and Service Delivery Models in Transgender Health.* The Lancet 388 (10042), 01–11.

Wylie, K., Barrett, J., Besser, M., Bouman, W.P., Bridgman, M., Clayton, A., Green, R., Hamilton, M., Hines, M., Ivbijaro, G., Khoosal, D., Lawrence, A., Lenihan, P., Loewenthal, D., Ralph, D., Reed, T., Stevens, J., Terry, T., Thom, B., Thornton, J., Walsh, D. & Ward, D. (2014). *Good practice guidelines for the assessment & treatment of adults with gender dysphoria.* Sexual & Relationship Therapy. 29, 2, 154–214.

INDEX

the *Shaw* **mind**
FOUNDATION

Supporting children, adults and families
for better mental health. **#lets**do**stuff**

Sign up to our charity, The Shaw Mind Foundation
www.shawmindfoundation.org
and keep in touch with us; we would love to hear from you.

*Our goal is to make help and support available for every
single person in society, from all walks of life.
We will never stop offering hope. These are our promises.*